The Voyage of King Njoya's Gift

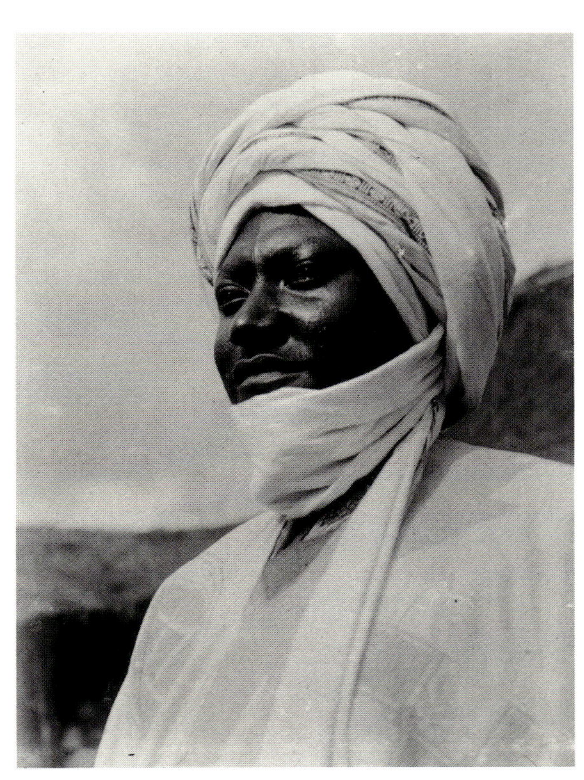

The Voyage of *King Njoya's Gift*

A Beaded Sculpture from the Bamum Kingdom, Cameroon, in the National Museum of African Art

Christraud M. Geary

National Museum of African Art
Smithsonian Institution

This publication was made possible in part by a generous grant from the Shell Oil Company Foundation.

Distributed by the University of Washington Press,
PO Box 50096, Seattle, Washington 98145

Library of Congress Cataloging-in-Publication Data
Geary, Christraud M.
The voyage of King Njoya's gift: a beaded sculpture from the Bamum Kingdom, Cameroon, in the National Museum of African Art, Smithsonian Institution, Washington, D.C. / Christraud M. Geary.
p. cm.
Includes bibliographical references.
ISBN 0-295-97428-1
1. Sculpture, Bamum. 2. Sculpture, Black—Cameroon. 3. Sculpture, Primitive—Cameroon. 4. Wood-carving, Bamun. 5. Wood-carving—Cameroon. 6. Beadwork—Cameroon. 7. Sculpture—Washington (D.C.) 8. Wood-carving—Washington (D.C.) 9. National Museum of African Art (U.S.) I. National Museum of African Art (U.S.) II. Title.
NB1255.C17G43 1994 730'.89'9636—dc20 94-38694
CIP

Editor: Joan Amick
Designer: Susan Cook

Cover
King Njoya in the central hall of the palace he built in 1917
Photograph by Anna Wuhrmann, 1920-21
Courtesy Basel Mission Archive, Basel, Switzerland; No. QE-30.006.0032

Inside cover
Male figure (detail of neck ornament)
Photograph by Franko Khoury

Half title page
Portrait of King Njoya
Photograph by Anna Wuhrmann, ca. 1912
Courtesy Basel Mission Archive, Basel, Switzerland; No. E-30.29.4,25

Figure 1 (opposite)
Male figure
19th century
Bamum peoples, Fumban, Grassfields region, Cameroon
Wood, brass, cloth, glass beads, cowrie shells
160 cm (63 in)
Gift of Evelyn A. J. Hall and John A. Friede, 85-8-1
Photograph by Franko Khoury
National Museum of African Art

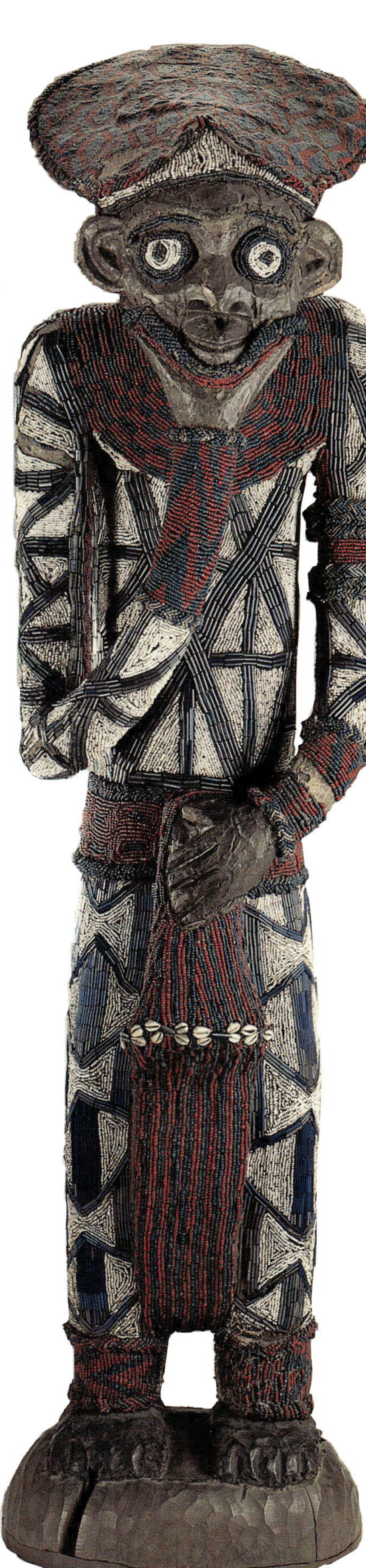

Contents

Acknowledgments

Scholarly projects extending over long periods of time often involve research in many places and investigation of myriad materials. My study of a beaded figure from the Bamum kingdom in Cameroon is an example of such an undertaking. It led me from Bamum, where I conducted fieldwork, to archives and museums in Cameroon, Switzerland, Germany, Austria, and France. As in a puzzle, the bits and pieces of information I have gathered over many years now fit into place to reveal the history of the figure that I present in this publication.

Along the way, institutions and individuals have helped me identify and place the pieces of this puzzle through their invaluable information, expertise, and generous support. First and foremost, I should mention the late ruler of the Bamum kingdom, His Majesty El Hadj Seidou Njimoluh Njoya, who, in 1977, opened the doors of the Palace Museum to me so that I could conduct research funded through a grant of the German Ministry for Foreign Affairs. Many members of the royal court, among them most notably the late Prince Yerima Jean, participated in the project. His Majesty El Hadj Ibrahim Mbombo Njoya, who succeeded El Hadj Seidou Njimoluh Njoya in 1992, took an interest in this project and allowed me to publish several photographs of objects in the Palace Museum. A grant of the Deutsche Forschungsgemeinschaft supported return trips to Bamum in 1983 and 1984 during which His Excellency Dr. Adamou Ndam Njoya and Dr. Aboubakar Njiassé-Njoya offered me further insight into the history and culture of the Bamum.

I am indebted to many colleagues who contributed ideas, allowed me to consult materials under their care, and offered me the use of photographs from their archives. Among them are Dr. Klaus Born, Völkerkundliche Sammlungen im Reiss-Museum, Mannheim (Germany); Dr. Doris Byer, Museum für Völkerkunde, Vienna (Austria); Professor Christopher DeCorse, Syracuse University (U.S.A.); Paul Jenkins, M.A., Basel Mission Archive, Basel (Switzerland); Dr. Hans-Joachim Koloss, Museum für Völkerkunde, Berlin (Germany); Professor Roy Sieber, Indiana University (U.S.A.); Dr. Angelika Tunis, Museum für Völkerkunde, Berlin (Germany), Professor Dr. Gisela Völger, Rautenstrauch-Joest Museum, Cologne (Germany); and Professor Claude Tardits, Paris (France). I would also like to thank Skip Palenik, who conducted the scientific analysis of the fabric that covers the figure. Finally, a grant from the American Council of Learned Societies supported research in the Zentrales Staatsarchiv, Potsdam (Germany) in 1990.

My father, Professor Günther W. Mühle, has been a very important participant in this research. Over the course of many years, he has transcribed German missionary and administrative documents on the Cameroon Grassfields, which were written in the old German script. Without these transcriptions, many of the documents presented here would not have been readily accessible.

Joan Amick, editor, and Susan Cook, designer—both staff members of the National Museum of African Art—were instrumental in creating the final form of this publication. I would like to thank them for their suggestions for improvement and patience throughout the project. Franko Khoury, photographer at the National Museum of African Art, put the figure into the right light and produced the first extensive visual record of the piece. Jo Moore provided the artwork for the map. My thanks go to all of them.

In conclusion, I would like to express my gratitude to Mrs. Sylvia H. Williams, Director of the National Museum of African Art. I greatly appreciate her insightful comments on the manuscript and thank her for the support and encouragement throughout the project.

Christraud M. Geary

Foreword

The National Museum of African Art has benefitted greatly from the generous private support of individuals, businesses, and foundations and from the public support of the federal government. This public-private partnership has made possible this publication devoted to an extraordinary beaded figure from Bamum, Cameroon, in the collection of the National Museum of African Art.

The sculpture was given to the museum by two donors, Evelyn A. J. Hall and John A. Friede, who have not only shared their appreciation of African visual traditions but have also continued the legacy of giving that brought this rare work of art from the kingdom of Bamum to the West. The earliest record of this piece identifies this figure as a gift; in 1908, Bamum's King Njoya gave the figure to the Glauning family in commemoration of his German friend and ally Captain Hans Glauning. In 1985, the figure was again a gift: from Evelyn A. J. Hall and John A. Friede to our national collection.

This essay reconstructs the unique history of this beaded figure and explores the cultural themes it embodies. We are deeply grateful to the Shell Oil Company Foundation for the generous grant that provided partial funding for this publication. Special thanks are also given to Dr. Christraud Geary, curator of the museum's Eliot Elisofon Photographic Archives; her meticulous scholarship, in conjunction with the years of research in Cameroon that have given her a special knowledge of the people and their remarkable traditions, has made this publication a reality.

The beaded figure from the kingdom of Bamum stands in proud testament to the creativity and skill of Bamum artists, to the rich fabric of their culture, and to the long-standing tradition of giving—a tradition that sustains our museum and enriches our many visitors.

Sylvia H. Williams
Director

Introduction

Among the works of art in the permanent collection of the National Museum of African Art, one object—a life-size male figure—stands out as a visually compelling masterpiece of beaded sculpture (Figs. 1–3). Bead embroidery covers most of the carved, wooden figure. On other areas—including the face, back of the head, hands, and feet—the artists applied a thin overlay of brass. At its base, the figure has a pole-like extension, which is not visible to the visitors of the gallery because of the way the sculpture is mounted in its case (Fig. 34). This extension suggests that the figure once may have been planted into the ground. This imposing sculpture comes from the Bamum kingdom located in the Grassfields region of what is now the Republic of Cameroon.

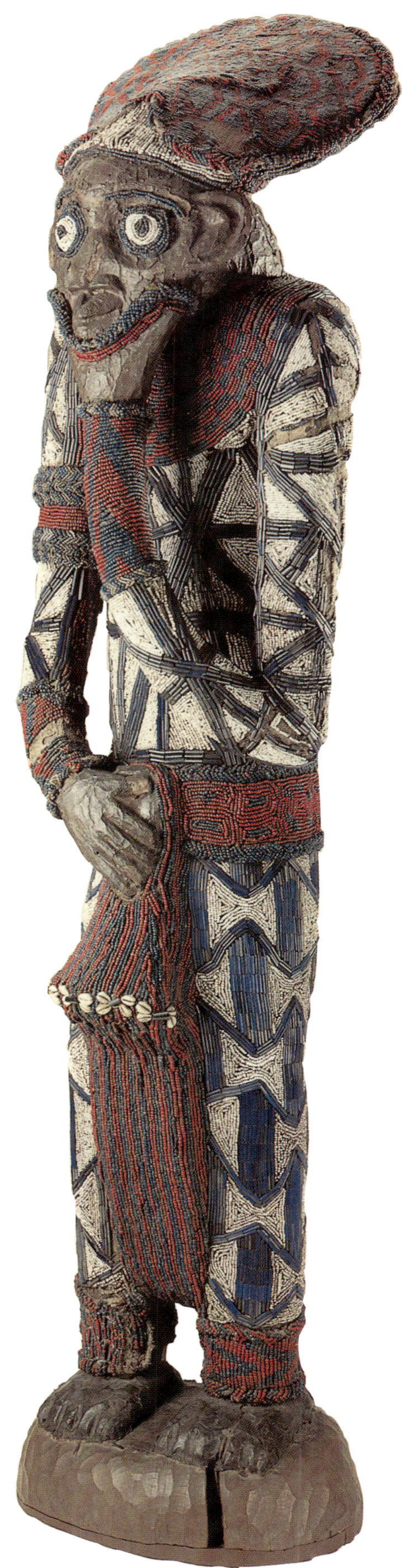

Figure 2
Male figure (3/4 left)
Photograph by Franko Khoury

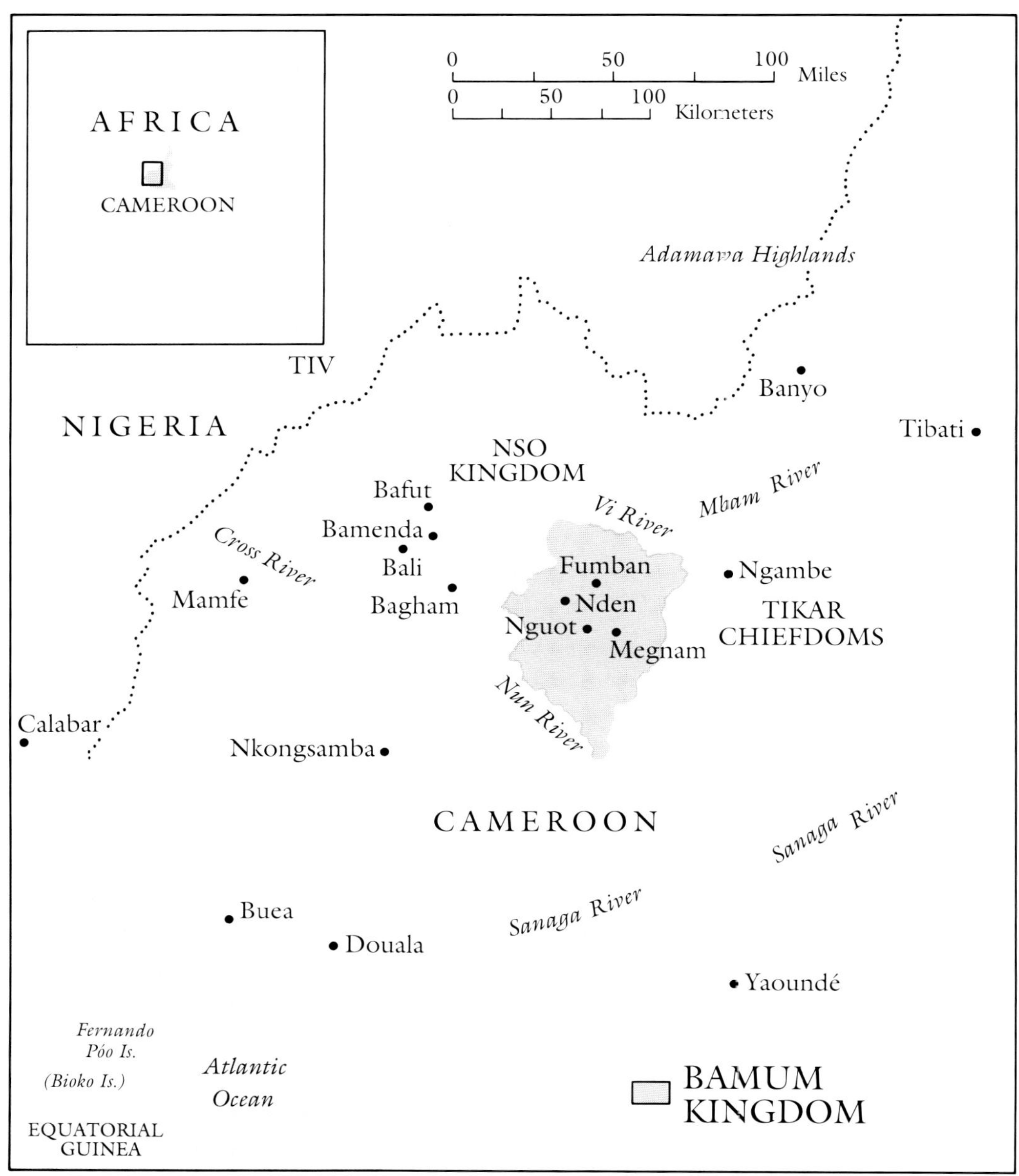

Map of the Bamum kingdom
by Jo Moore

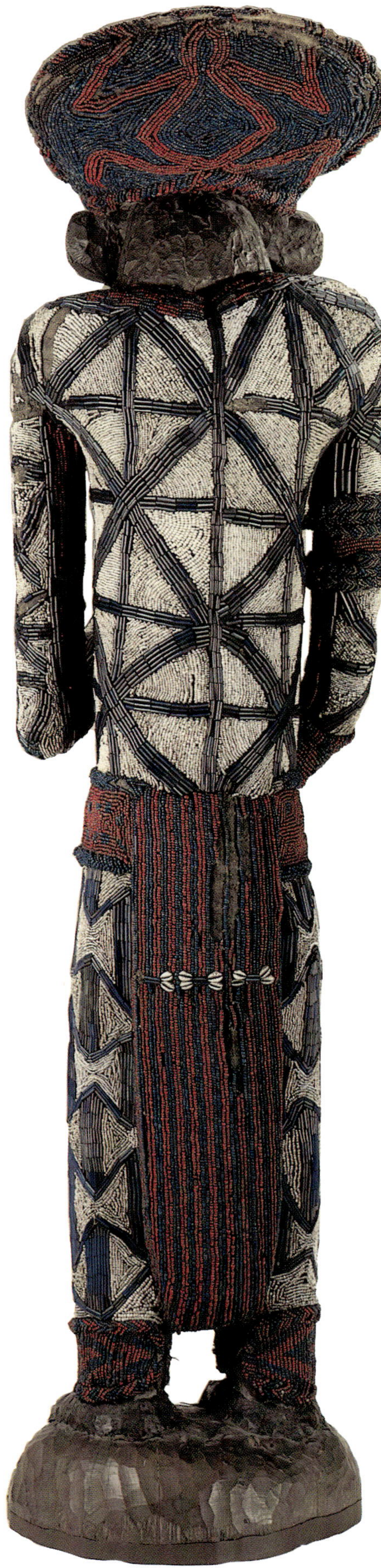

Several scholars have discussed the sculpture in their writings and have speculated about its age, history, iconography, and meaning. One interpretation assumes that the figure was the portrait of a German colonial officer and that it was produced in 1908 (see Northern 1984, 99–98; Harter 1986, 162 and Pl. 12; Perrois 1994, 44, 51). However, this interpretation—based on an incomplete reading of historical documents and a lack of detailed analysis of the figure's style, dress and adornment, and iconography—cannot be upheld.

The following essay presents the first full examination of this work of art. The first part discusses the history of the Bamum kingdom and the experience of the Bamum under German colonial rule. The second part of the essay is devoted to the figure's unique history, which was reconstructed through information from museum records, historical documents, and letters. Drawing on knowledge of Bamum culture and of the history of Bamum art and artistic expression, the third part of this essay addresses the figure's physical properties, such as the materials used in its production, and its stylistic characteristics;[1] it then interprets the sculpture's iconography. Some of the most difficult questions pertaining to the figure's function and meaning will be raised in the final part of the essay.

Figure 3
Male figure (back)
Photograph by Franko Khoury

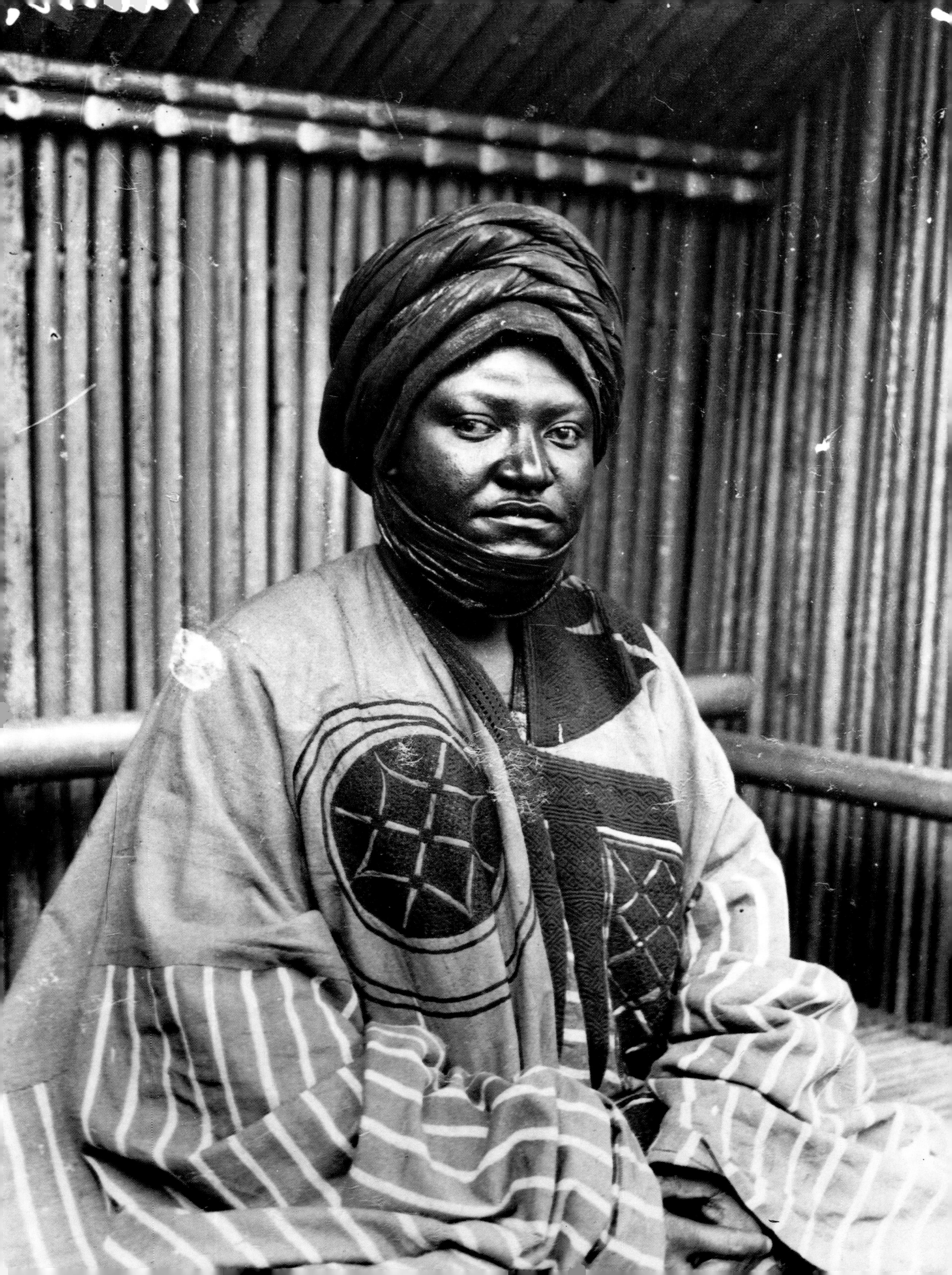

The Bamum Kingdom

The Bamum kingdom, where artists created this sculpture, is the largest among the many kingdoms in the Grassfields region of western Cameroon. The present Bamum king, His Majesty El Hadj Ibrahim Mbombo Njoya, who has ruled since 1992, resides in the palace at Fumban, the kingdom's capital. He is the nineteenth ruler of this ancient state, which was founded approximately four hundred years ago when a prince, Nshare Yen, and his followers defeated populations in the region of Fumban and established their rule (*Histoire* 1952, 22–24; Tardits 1980, 97–126). At the beginning of the twentieth century, Ibrahim Njoya (ca. 1873–1933), portrayed in Figure 4, was the charismatic ruler of the kingdom, which then comprised approximately eight thousand square kilometers (3,090 square miles)—more than twice the area of Rhode Island—and had an estimated seventy thousand inhabitants (Tardits 1980, 922).

At the turn of this century, the Bamum state was highly stratified. At the apex of society stood the king (*mfon*), who was the political and military leader. He acted as the supreme mediator between the living and the ancestors. He surrounded himself with members of the royal family and noble men who held high offices and served as his retainers and advisors. The royalty and nobility, approximately one-third of the population, formed the upper echelon of Bamum society. Two-thirds of the kingdom's inhabitants belonged to the workforce and had few privileges. They worked in the plantations of the noblemen, who sent to the court annual tributes, which the king redistributed. The king also controlled access to imported goods, such as brass and glass beads, and his monopoly extended to the domain of the arts. The king not only regulated certain materials used in the production of artworks but also determined which iconographic motifs were reserved for royalty and which could be displayed by the larger populace.

Figure 4
King Njoya
Photograph by Marie-Pauline Thorbecke, January 1912
Courtesy Rautenstrauch-Joest-Museum Cologne, Germany; No. 19333

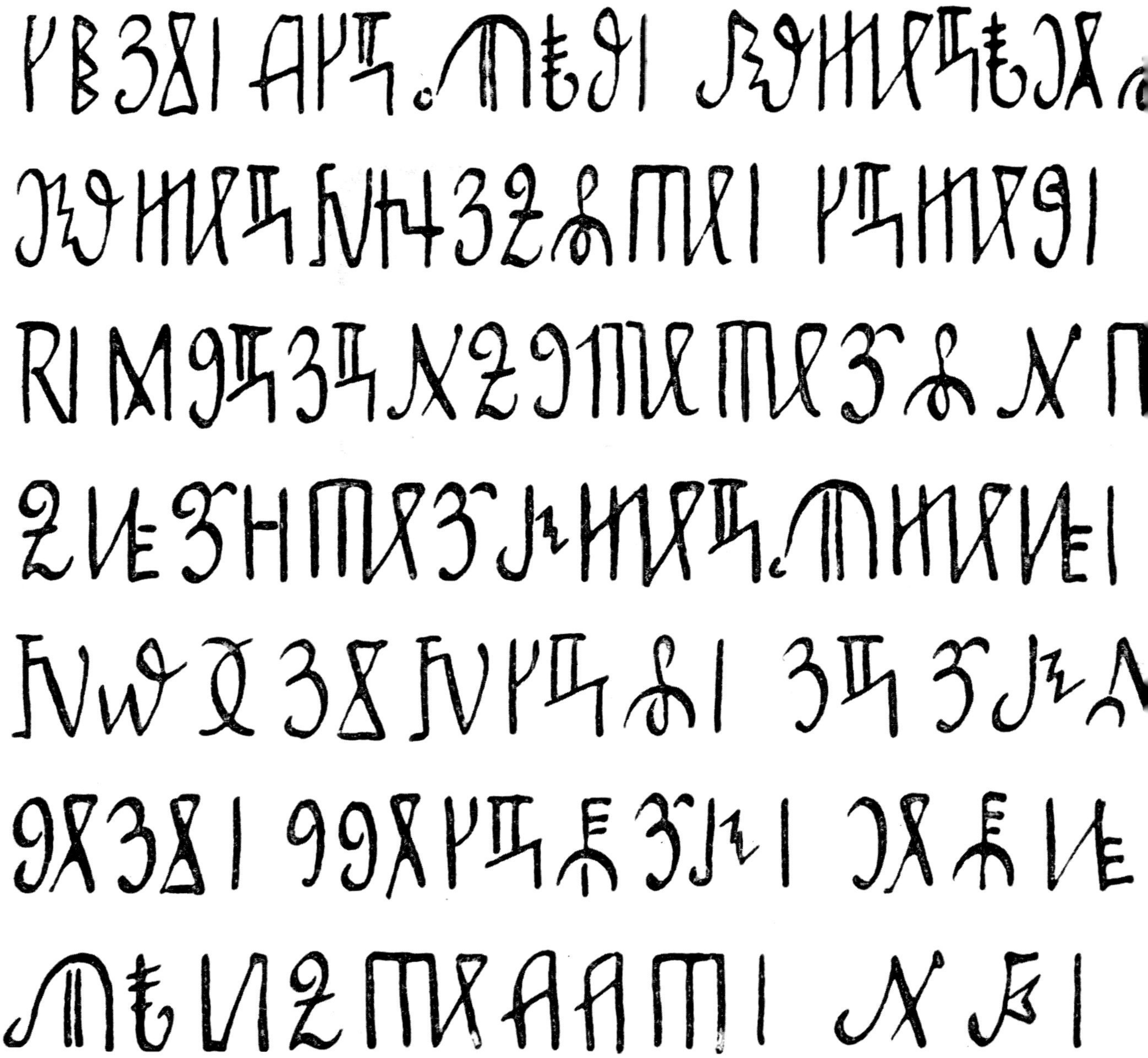

Several European and Bamum scholars have studied the history of the Bamum kingdom.[2] It is, however, one of the most fortuitous coincidences of African historiography that we also have King Njoya's own account of the intricate history of the kingdom.

During the last years of the nineteenth century, Njoya and his courtiers, inspired by Arabic script, invented a system of writing the Bamum language (Fig. 5). Initially including approximately five hundred pictograms, their written language underwent several transformations before the final alphabet emerged in 1916 (Tardits 1980, 38–9; Tardits 1991). In 1910 or 1911, Njoya and his courtiers began to compile the history of the Bamum kingdom.[3] The writing and editing took many years and was finally completed in 1931 (Tardits 1980, 41). In these extraordinary chronicles, the king and his loyal servants presented the history of the Bamum kings and events from the founding of the Bamum kingdom through the German and French colonial periods.[4] They also noted the history of many neighboring kingdoms. In 1952, this unique work appeared in a

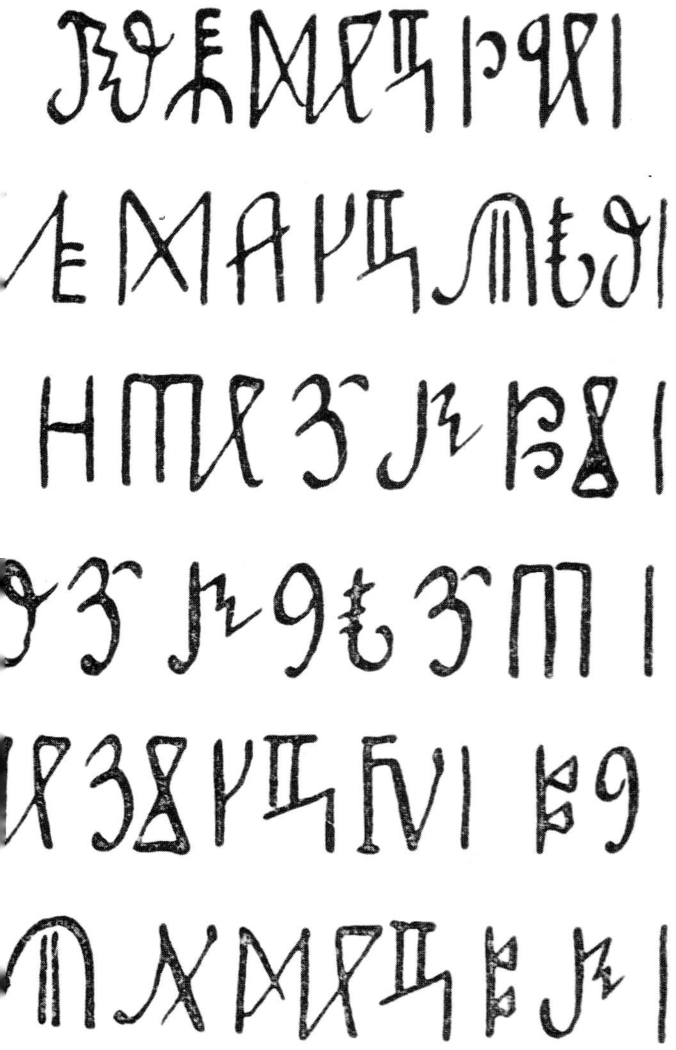

Figure 5
The Lord's Prayer in Bamum script
Written in 1911, the prayer is an example of a revised version of the Bamum alphabet. The script is called "a ka ku u ku," a name derived from its first four characters (Rein-Wuhrmann 1925, 115).

French translation entitled *Histoire et coutumes des Bamum*. From these sources, the history of Bamum—particularly the years of King Njoya's rule—can be reconstructed in great detail.

King Njoya became ruler of Bamum in his early teens—sometime between 1885 and 1887—after his father, King Nsangu (ruled ca. 1865–72 to ca. 1885–87),[5] and many Bamum soldiers were killed during a battle with the neighboring Nso peoples (*Histoire* 1952, 151–56; Tardits 1980, 195–98, 919). A long-time rival of the Bamum, the Nso competed with them for control of territory and trade routes. The Bamum had invaded the kingdom of Nso in order to expand their sphere of influence. In this particular battle, the Nso withstood the Bamum attack. In fact, the Nso not only won the battle, but they also retained the head of the deceased king and thereby denied him a proper Bamum funeral. Without the official royal burial of his predecessor, Njoya's succession was not sanctioned.

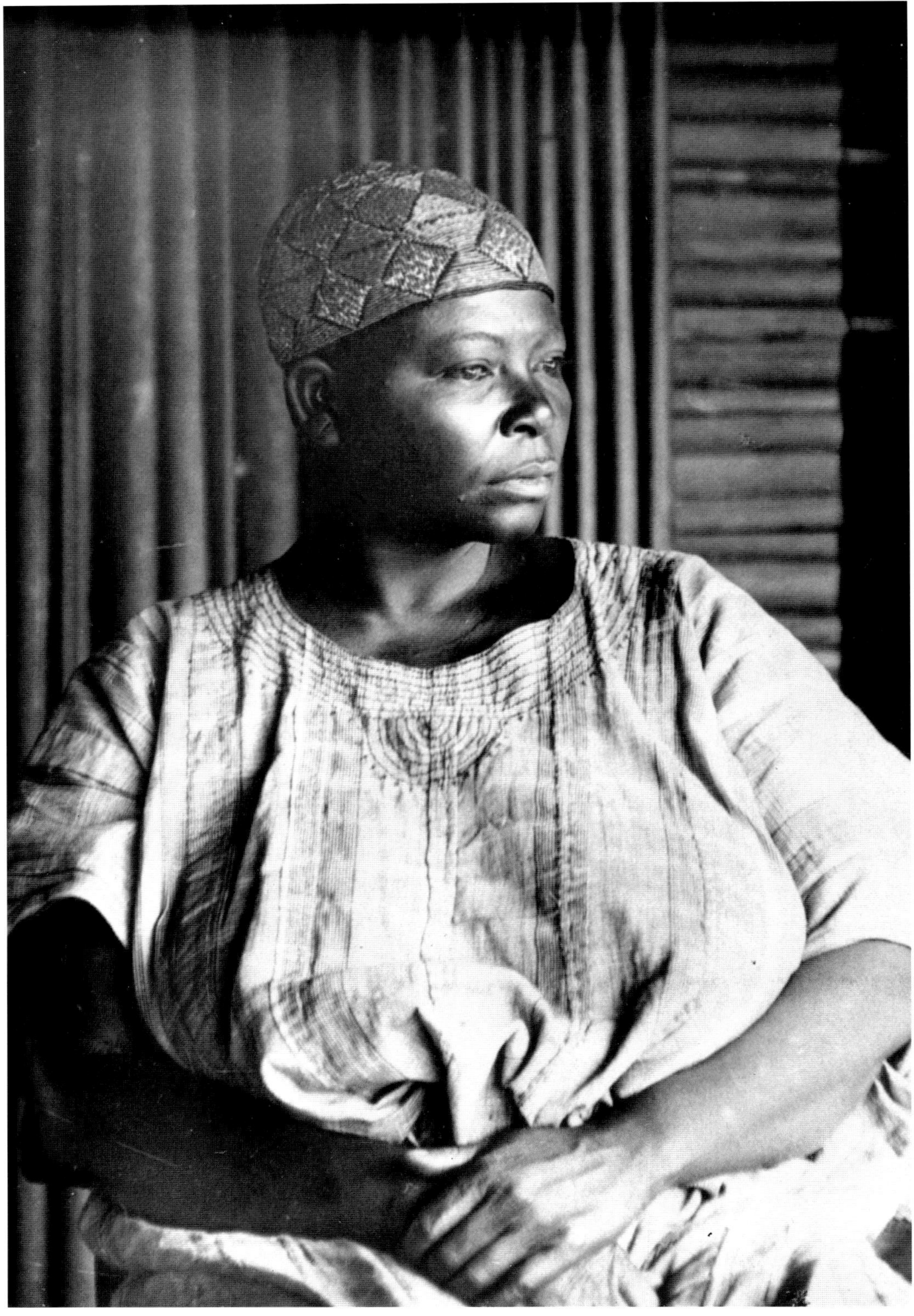

Figure 6
Queen Mother Njapundunke
Photograph by Bernhard Ankermann, April–May 1908
Courtesy Museum für Völkerkunde Berlin, Germany; No. VIII A 5426

Initially, Njoya's energetic mother, Queen Njapundunke (who died in 1913), held the reins of the kingdom (Fig. 6). During the early years of his rule, young Njoya and his mother faced external threats and internal unrest. In 1894, Gbetnkom Ndombua, an influential royal servant, tried to usurp power by instigating a revolt. Unable to muster enough support inside the kingdom, Njoya appealed to Lamido Umaru, the ruler of the neighboring Fulbe kingdom of Banyo, for help. Banyo was one of the southernmost Islamic states in what is now the Republic of Cameroon. Between 1895 and 1897, mounted Fulbe troops from Banyo suppressed the uprising and safeguarded Njoya's rule. In return for the military support, he showered the Lamido with presents (*Histoire* 1952, 39). Njoya and his court also converted to Islam, adopted Islamic clothing, established a cavalry, and began to model themselves after their Islamic neighbors (Njiassé-Njoya 1981, 49–81).

Forming alliances with outside powers to protect his kingdom and interests was Njoya's strategy during most of his reign. He saw himself as a mediator and as a politician who worked within given realities. Yet, he never lost sight of his goal: to maintain and consolidate the Bamum kingdom in face of external changes, turmoil, even intervention. His greatest challenge, however, was yet to come.

As a result of the Berlin Conference (1884–85),[6] the territory that is now the Republic of Cameroon came under German colonial domination. In the years that followed,

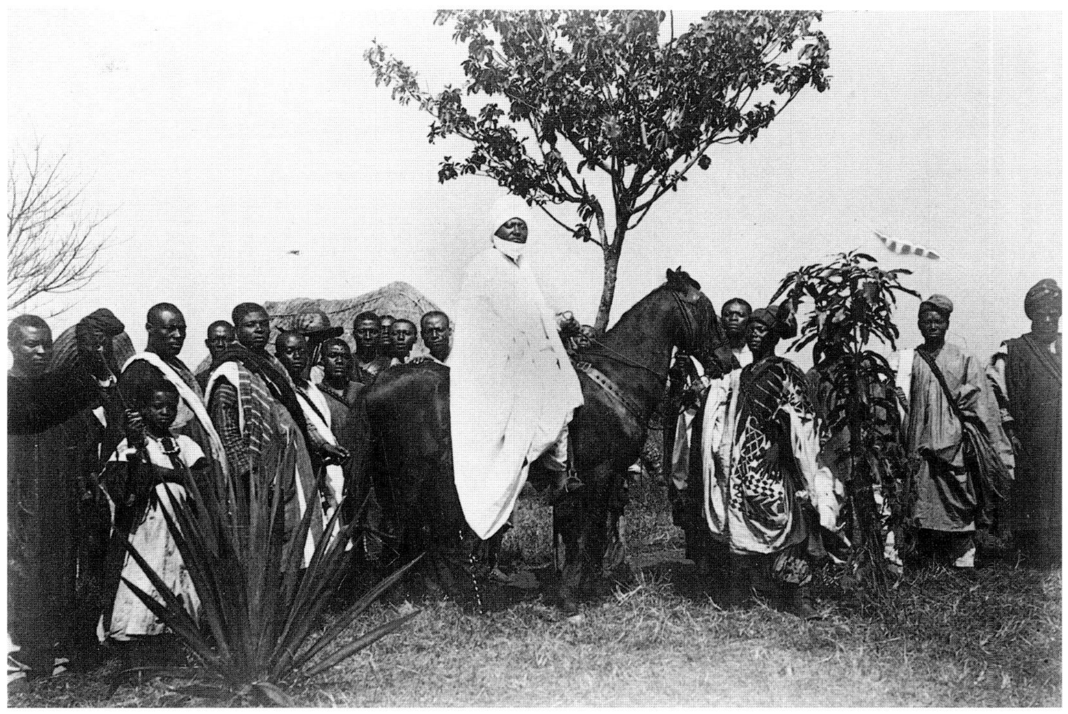

Figure 7
King Njoya on horseback
Photograph possibly by Anna Wuhrmann or Eugen Schwarz, ca. 1912
Courtesy Basel Mission Archive, Basel, Switzerland; No. E-30.29.068

German military, travelers, and merchants explored, conquered, and exploited the colony as they established themselves in all parts of Cameroon. In 1902, the first Germans—a military officer and two representatives of trading companies—accompanied by African soldiers, arrived in the Bamum kingdom (Sandrock 1902). In the Bamum chronicles, King Njoya and his courtiers describe their initial reaction to the foreign intruders.

> One day, the whites appeared in the country; the Bamum said to themselves: "Let us fight them."—No! said Njoya, because I have seen in a dream that the whites did not do anything bad to the Bamum. If the Bamum would fight them, it would not only be directed against their people ... but also against my own. There would be very few Bamum survivors; this would not be good." He, Njoya, ripped the arrows, lances and guns out of their hands. The Bamum obeyed, and did not oppose the arrival of the whites. He, Njoya, helped the Bamum and they remained in peace. (*Histoire* 1952, 134; translated from French)[7]

Njoya thus decided on a policy of accommodation and of careful diplomacy because he anticipated that opposition to the Germans might have negative consequences for the future of his kingdom (*Histoire* 1952, 42).

As a result of King Njoya's deliberate strategy, Bamum became one of the principal allies of the Germans and thrived. Indeed, during the German colonial period, which officially ended in 1916, King Njoya's policy of accommodation allowed him to remain autonomous and to minimize German interference in Bamum affairs. During the German colonial presence, King Njoya thus experienced the grand years of his rule (Tardits 1980, 218). As Njoya states in the chronicle:

> The Germans did Njoya well. They let him have all the power to rule all of the land of the Bamum. While he governed the country, there was disorder neither with the whites nor with the Bamum. (*Histoire* 1952, 134; translated from French)

In the eyes of German colonial officials and the public, the kingdom of Bamum was a well-organized African state ruled by an enlightened king (Geary 1988, 47–61). Bamum became known for its splendid court arts—including masks, beaded stools, brass and bead jewelry, elaborate ceremonial terra-cotta pipes, and intricately ornamented swords—which attracted German collectors. When the directors and curators in German ethnographic museums heard of the exquisite objects from the Bamum palace, they sent their agents to Bamum. They also enlisted the help of the colonial military to bring Bamum art to their museums.

Njoya was aware of the Germans' interest in these works. Once again, he engaged in a well-contemplated strategy. He often gave valuable gifts to high-ranking German officials and Emperor Wilhelm II (1859–1941). His most famous gift is a two-figure throne, which he sent to the German Emperor in 1908. The throne is now one of the masterpieces in the Museum für Völkerkunde in Berlin (Geary 1981; Geary 1983a). In return, Njoya received gifts from German officials. These exchanges resembled the gift-giving transactions between important kings of the Grassfields region that reinforced political alliances as well as cordial relationships (Warnier 1985, 262–69).[8] In addition, King Njoya allowed the sale of selected pieces; he determined which works could be sold and how much they should cost.[9]

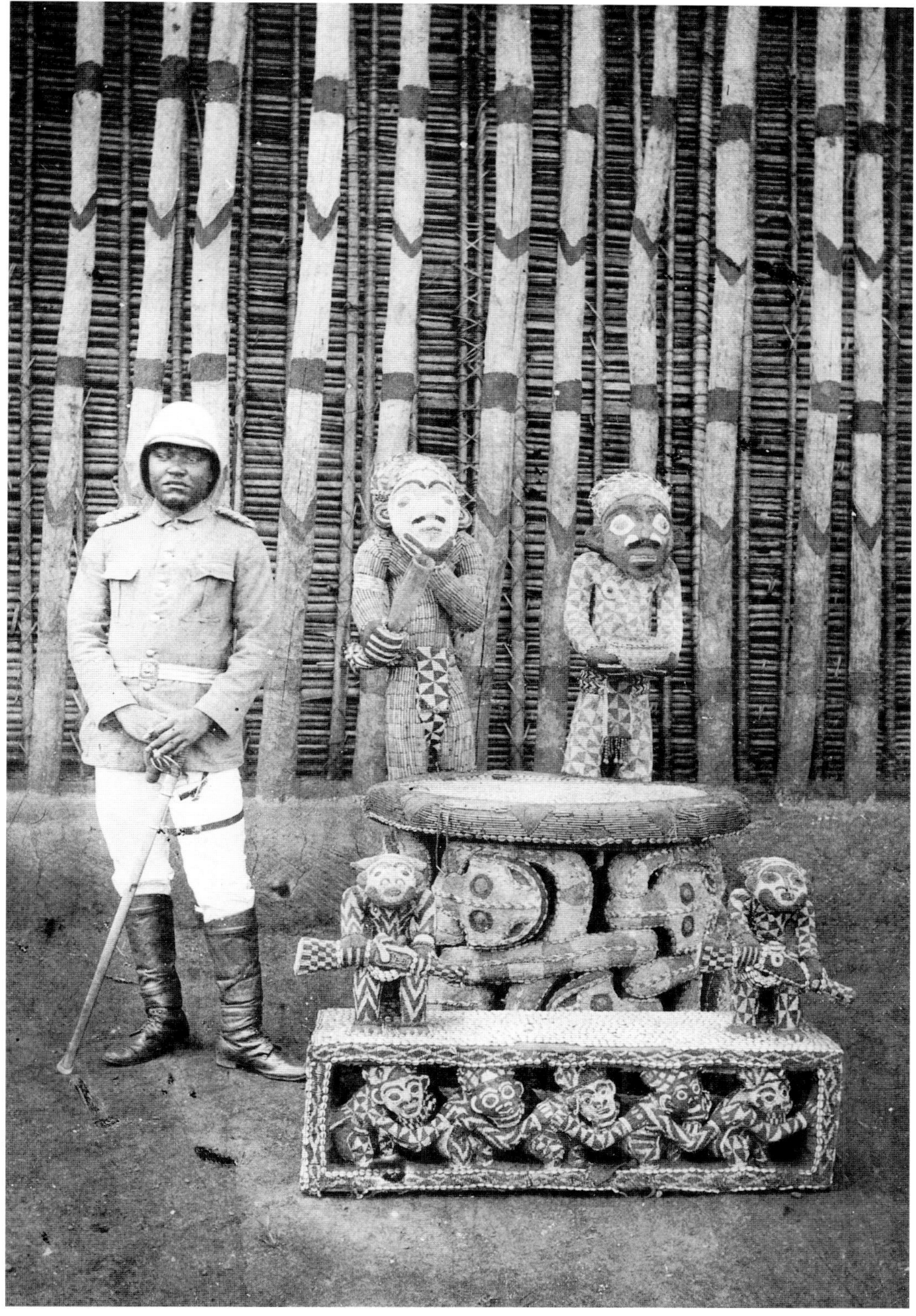

Figure 8
King Njoya and his father's throne in front of a palace that was built in 1905
Photograph by Martin Göhring, November 1905
Courtesy Basel Mission Archive, Basel, Switzerland; No. E-30.29.042

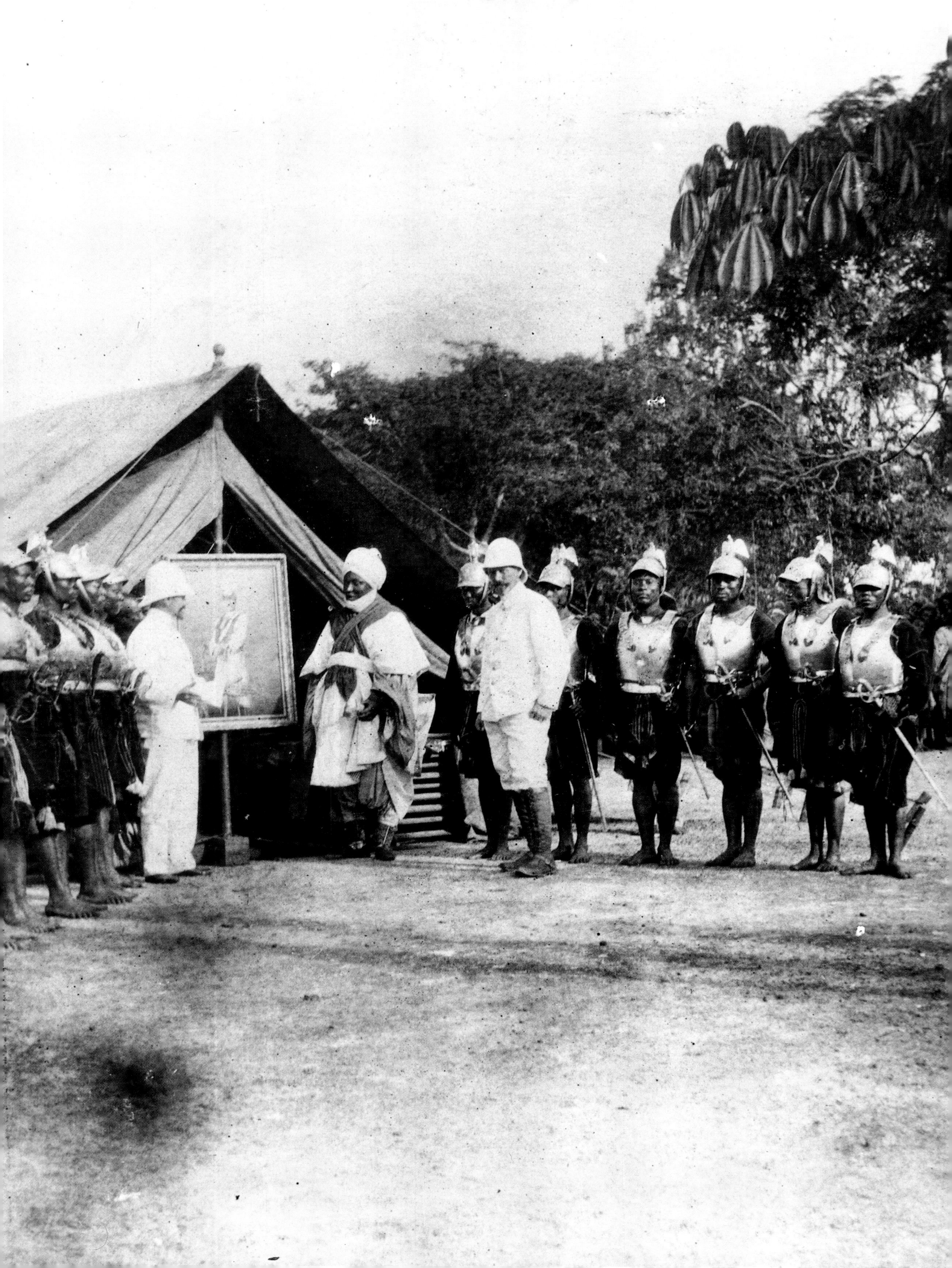

The History of the Figure

The King and the German Officer

In this setting, a most unusual relationship between King Njoya and a German military officer, Hauptmann (Captain) Hans Glauning (1868–1908), developed. From 1894, Glauning (Fig. 10) lived in German East Africa and Cameroon; he assumed command of the German military station at Bamenda in 1905 ("Zwei Trauerbotschaften" 1908). Bamum belonged to the Bamenda military district and was thus administered through Bamenda.

According to his writings, Glauning respected King Njoya, the consummate politician.[10] Glauning's special role, as well as his sympathy and admiration for the Bamum ruler, granted him access to the Bamum court. Among the Bamum, Glauning enjoyed the reputation of a tough but fair administrator and military man. In several instances, Glauning came to Njoya's and his mother's aid when German merchants harassed Bamum royal women (*Histoire* 1952, 75). Additionally, there were frequent conflicts between the merchants and the king because he was expected to provide them with Bamum porters to carry their goods to the Cameroon coast. In June 1907, Glauning traveled to Fumban to mediate between the king and merchants ("Abschrift" 1907a; "Abschrift" 1907b).

In 1906, the German military under Captain Glauning's command and Bamum soldiers under Njoya's leadership undertook a victorious campaign against the Nso, the ancient enemy of the Bamum (H. Glauning 1906a). The Nso had opposed German rule and suffered severe repercussions. The alliance with the Germans endowed King Njoya with the power to avenge his father (*Histoire* 1952, 135). The German Lieutenant von

Figure 9
King Njoya receiving a portrait of Emperor Wilhelm II for his support of the German military campaign against the Nso kingdom
Photograph possibly by Lieutenant von Putlitz or Martin Göhring, 1906
Courtesy Linden-Museum Stuttgart, Germany; No. Kam 201

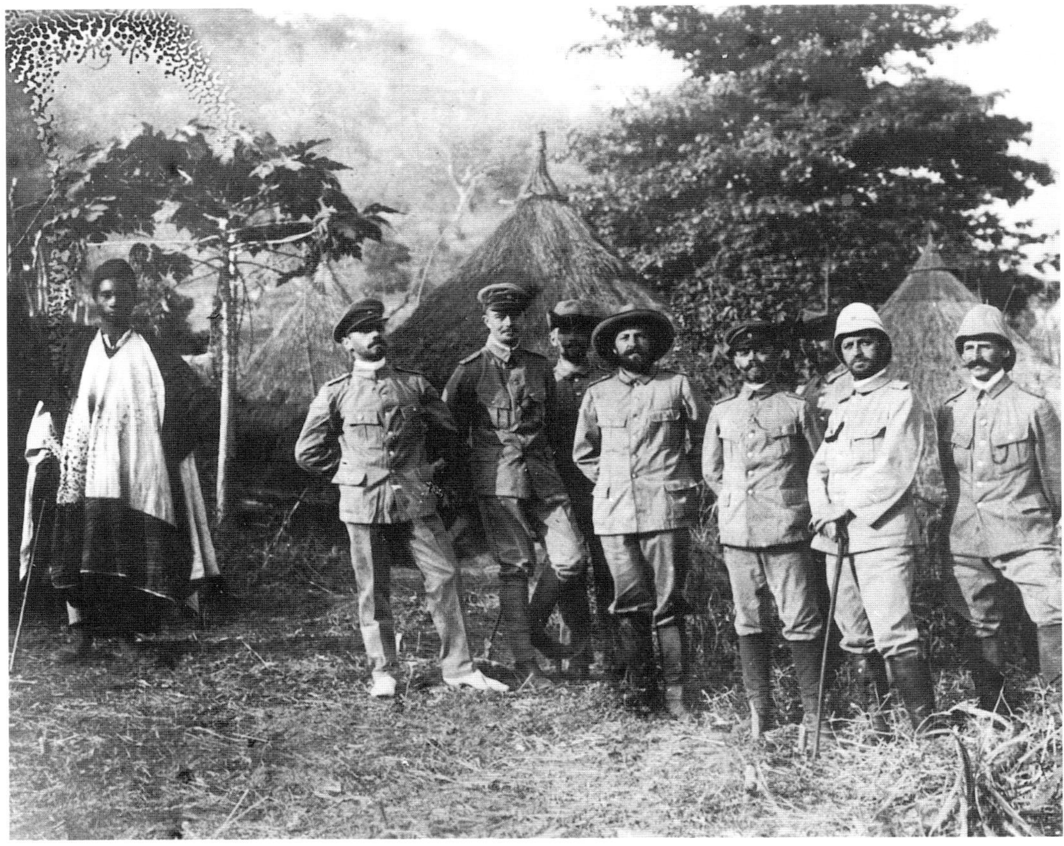

Figure 10
German military men
Captain Hans Glauning is the second from the left.
Photographer unknown, ca. 1905
Courtesy Museum für Völkerkunde Berlin, Germany; No. VIII A 959

Wenckstern was able to recover King Nsangu's head, which had been in the possession of the Nso king since 1885–87.[11] A moving account preserved in the German Zentrales Staatsarchiv at Potsdam and in an abbreviated article that appeared in the *Deutsches Kolonialblatt* details the return of King Nsangu's head to Bamum ("Abschrift" 1906; Wenckstern 1907). The sight of the head, which von Wenckstern presented to King Njoya, moved the ruler and his loyal retainers to tears. Thereafter, King Nsangu received the proper royal funerary rites that legitimized King Njoya's rule. Germans and Bamum celebrated the victory over the Nso in Fumban, the capital of the Bamum kingdom. For his services, King Njoya was given a medal and a portrait of German Emperor Wilhelm II (Fig. 9).[12] Njoya and the editors mention this event in their chronicles. Although the Bamum authors rarely give the names of German officials, they refer to Captain Glauning in this context.

> But he, Njoya took vengeance for these dead, by triumphing of the Nso. Hauptmann Grared[13] awarded the king a medal and said that he was a valiant man, as were the Bamum, too. (*Histoire* 1952, 135; translated from French)

Like many military men in the German colonies in Africa, Glauning collected African objects. Over the years, he became one of the most important suppliers of the Museum für Völkerkunde in Berlin. Among the members of the museum's staff, Glauning had an excellent reputation for his keen eye and his loyalty to the museum. He frequently corresponded with the director of the museum, Felix von Luschan (1854–1924). Most of this correspondence is now in the museum's archives.[14] Bernhard Ankermann (1857–1943), an ethnologist and assistant at the museum, was also familiar with the growing Glauning collection. The museum's close relationship with Glauning may have influenced Ankermann's decision to conduct anthropological fieldwork in the Grassfields region of Cameroon beginning in October 1907 (Baumann and Vajda 1959).

Glauning also sent objects to his family in Plauen, in the then kingdom of Saxony, Germany. Some of these objects were actually destined for the Berlin museum, as is evident from Glauning's correspondence. In fact, in a letter written in November 1907, Glauning indicated that, in case of his death, particular pieces should go to Berlin.[15]

It seems as if this letter had been a premonition; Captain Glauning died in action three and a half months later on March 5, 1908. The news of his death traveled quickly through the colony to Germany. Ankermann was in Bali near Bamenda when the news reached him. In a letter to Felix von Luschan, he wrote:

> You may already have received the sad news about Captain Glauning's death. We received it on the 13th [of March] through an express courier from Bamenda. I could not go over there for the funeral, since it already took place the same morning. He was killed in action on the 5th [of March], apparently by a shot in the head. He was killed instantly. His death is mourned by everybody, by whites and natives. (Ankermann 1908a; translated from German)

Perhaps the most extraordinary expression of this sentiment came from King Njoya. In memory of his friend and ally, he sent the life-size, beaded sculpture that is now in the permanent collection of the National Museum of African Art to Bamenda Station (Figs. 1–3). In April 1908, Lieutenant von der Planitz, the interim station commander, received the gift and informed von Luschan in a letter:

> We have here still a number of loads of curiosities from Captain Glauning, among them several from the Muntschi[16] expedition [during which he was killed]. In addition, a large figure, which Njoya sent, in order to plant it on the grave or to transmit it to Glauning's next of kin. (Planitz 1908; translated from German)

This first written reference to the figure explains how the sculpture left Bamum. King Njoya sent it as a royal gift in commemoration of his ally. This unusual gesture symbolically concluded the relationship between the two men who had appreciated and respected one another.

The Sculpture's Voyage

The news of Glauning's death set into motion a flurry of activities at the Berlin museum. The plan was to acquire everything that Glauning had not yet donated or sold to the museum. Ankermann, who had arrived in Bamum at the at the end of March 1908, was dispatched to Bamenda to evaluate the collection of objects, including the figure King Njoya had given to the Glauning family, held at the military station. At the same time, von Luschan contacted Hermann Glauning, one of the deceased's brothers. Von Luschan later informed the family that the museum intended to dedicate a hall to Glauning in the building they were planning to construct (Luschan 1908a). In a note on the margin of this document—dated April 30, 1908—von Luschan remarks that Hermann Glauning paid him a personal visit and that the family plans to sell the estate. Ankermann, in a letter of May 15, 1908, described the collection at Bamenda station and suggested that the museum should pay for its transport to Germany. He concluded that the collection was well worth this expense:

> The life-size, bead-covered grave figure alone, which King Njoya has sent—a great rarity for Bamum—almost makes up for the cost. (Ankermann 1908b; translated from German)

In July of 1908, the family—represented by Dr. Fritz Glauning, a relative and municipal judge—and the museum agreed that all objects still in Bamenda Station should be shipped to Germany and that the museum would pay for the transport (F. Glauning 1908a). From this collection, the family was to select several pieces that it would keep.[17] It was no doubt von Luschan's hope that the family would give or sell the majority of the collection to the museum. This proved to be the case.

In light of von Luschan's promise to dedicate a hall to Glauning, the family members were interested in selling most of the estate to the Berlin museum. They even considered allowing the museum to sell or exchange those pieces in the collection that it did not intend to keep (F. Glauning 1908b). This permission by the family would prove to be of crucial importance to the museum and would direct the ultimate destinations of some of the objects.

By November 1908, the transaction was completed. In a letter to Ankermann in Bamum, von Luschan wrote from Berlin:

> During these days, the negotiations with Glauning's heirs have come to a conclusion. We have to pay a total of 7000 marks, which, in my opinion, seems quite a bit; but the heirs had also approached other museums and one of those, I think Leipzig, has then pushed up the price. However, we now have secured our dominant position in regards to Northwest Cameroon. (Luschan 1908b; translated from German)

Soon thereafter, both parts of the estate—the objects from Bamenda and the holdings in Plauen—became part of the Berlin museum's collections.

King Njoya's generous gift, the large beaded figure, was one of the most important pieces in the Berlin museum. The first published report and photograph of the figure appeared in *Kolonie und Heimat* ("Ein seltsames Grabdenkmal" 1909). Photographs of the sculpture were subsequently published in several books, such as *Eine Reise durch die deutschen Kolonien* (1910) and Eckart von Sydow's *Handbuch der afrikanischen Plastik* (1930).[18] The Glauning hall and the new Museum für Völkerkunde never materialized, although Glauning's collections were held in high esteem. When the First World War brought an end to German colonial rule in Africa, collections from the colonies lost their immediate relevance (see Geary 1995). After the First World War, as the German economy fell on hard times and the financial situations of many museums became precarious, the museum at Berlin began to trade and sell objects in order to acquire others that would enrich its collections.

In March 1929, a committee of experts permitted the museum to trade the Bamum figure for ancient and precious jewelry given by the last king of the Aztec Empire to Hernan Cortés (1485–1547), the Spanish conqueror of Mexico, who in turn presented it to Emperor Charles V (1500–1558). Arthur Speyer, a German collector and dealer who had acquired this jewelry, offered it to the museum in exchange for the Bamum figure ("Report" 1929).[19] Speyer later sold the figure to a private British collector. It remained in England until it was acquired by two American collectors, Evelyn A. J. Hall and John A. Friede, who donated the figure to the National Museum of African Art in 1985. This donation concluded the unique voyage of this sculpture from the Bamum kingdom through Europe to the National Museum of African Art.

On following page, clockwise from upper left

Figure 11
Male figure (detail of upper right arm)
Photograph by Franko Khoury

Figure 12
Male figure (detail of back)
Photograph by Franko Khoury

Figure 13
Male figure (detail of belt)
Photograph by Franko Khoury

Figure 14
Male figure (detail of neck ornament)
Photograph by Franko Khoury

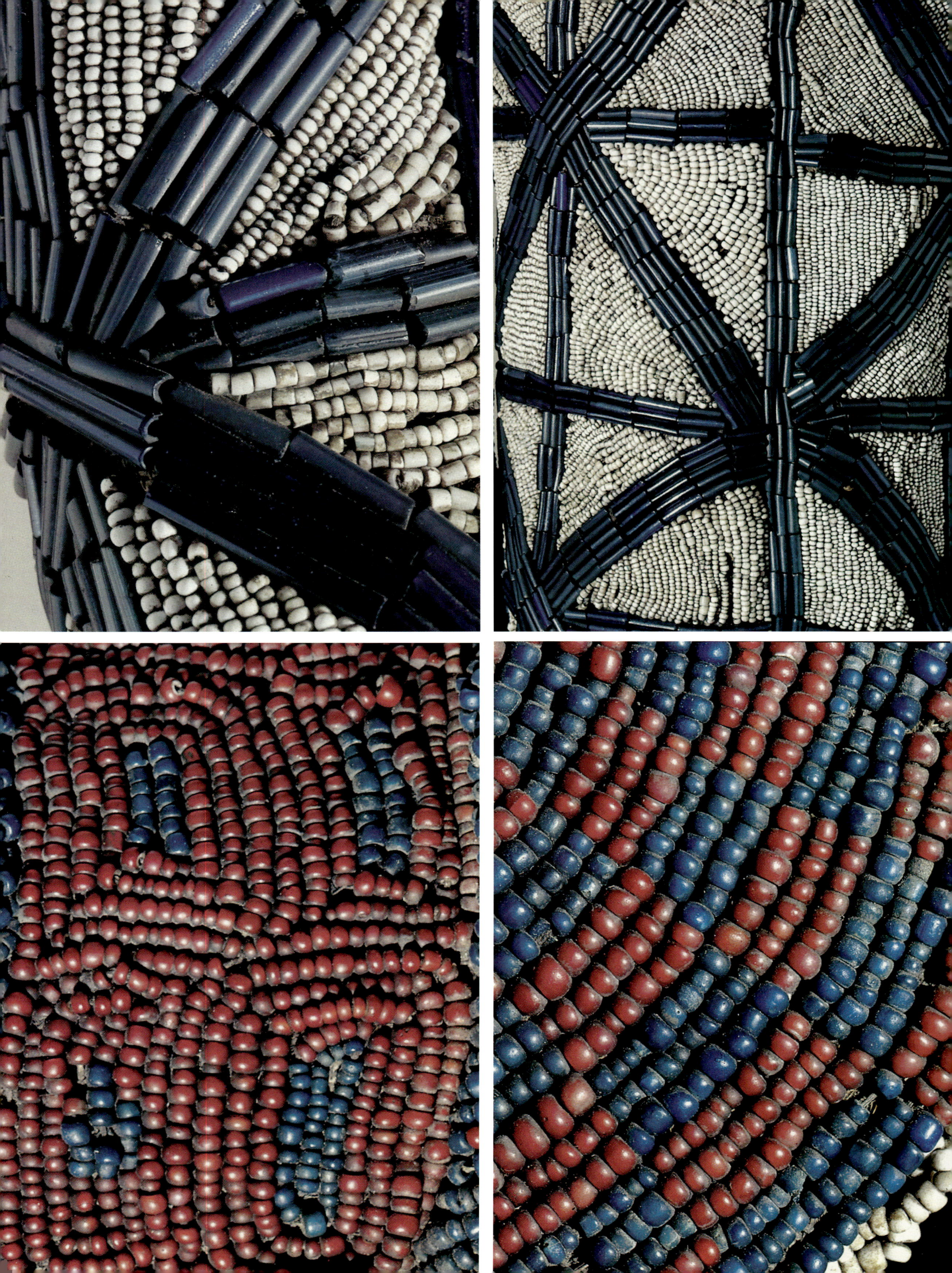

Examining the Sculpture

Production and Materials

Visual arts have always played a major role in the Bamum kingdom. During the nineteenth century, artists[20]—who specialized in carving, bead working, brass casting, pottery making, and weaving—worked exclusively for the king, the royal family, and members of the palace elite. Some of the most important artists originated from kingdoms the Bamum had subjugated during the expansion of their state. For their services, the rulers awarded them wives, clothing, and food.

Excellent bead artists came from Megnam, a subjugated kingdom southeast of Fumban. Some of the most prominent carvers and brass casters who worked for the king came from the small kingdom of Nguot. They belonged to the lineage of *Nji*[21] Nkome, who was a son of the chief of the Nguot. During the rule of Bamum King Mbuembue (ca. 1820–1840), one of the most charismatic leaders of the state, the Bamum defeated the Nguot and brought *Nji* Nkome to Fumban. His descendants now reside in Njinka, a quarter of the city located next to the palace. A successor of *Nji* Nkome—who, as is customary, assumed the same name—is said to have been the creator of the famous Bamum two-figure thrones in the second half of the nineteenth century. *Nji* Ase was another carver who worked at the turn of this century. His lineage hailed from the subjugated kingdom of Nden. However, there were also carvers who were members of the royal family; one of these, *Nji* Lu, was one of the principal artists at the palace and supervised the carvers during King Njoya's rule (see Geary 1983b, 86).

In the nineteenth century, beginning with Mbuembue's rule, artists of the palace created sculptures, masks, and beaded adornments, and the court arts proliferated. They flourished under King Nsangu in the 1870s and 1880s, when the artists produced large beaded thrones (Figs. 8, 17, 23), stools, and other sculptures. King Njoya continued these traditions during the first part of his reign in the 1890s. The presence of artists at the court, especially of those who came from subjugated kingdoms, signified the power of the Bamum rulers to control people and resources. Their splendid works thus attested

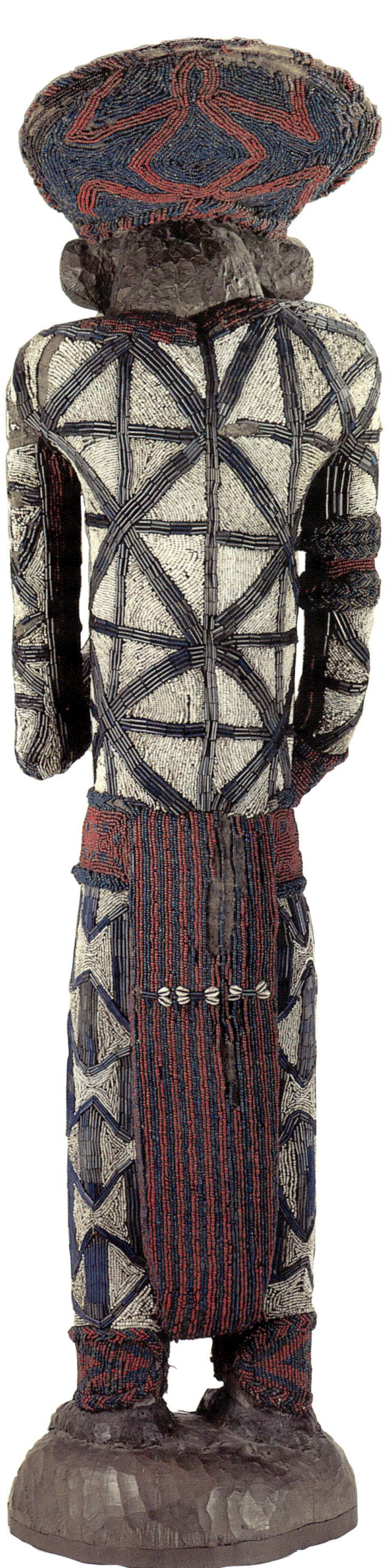

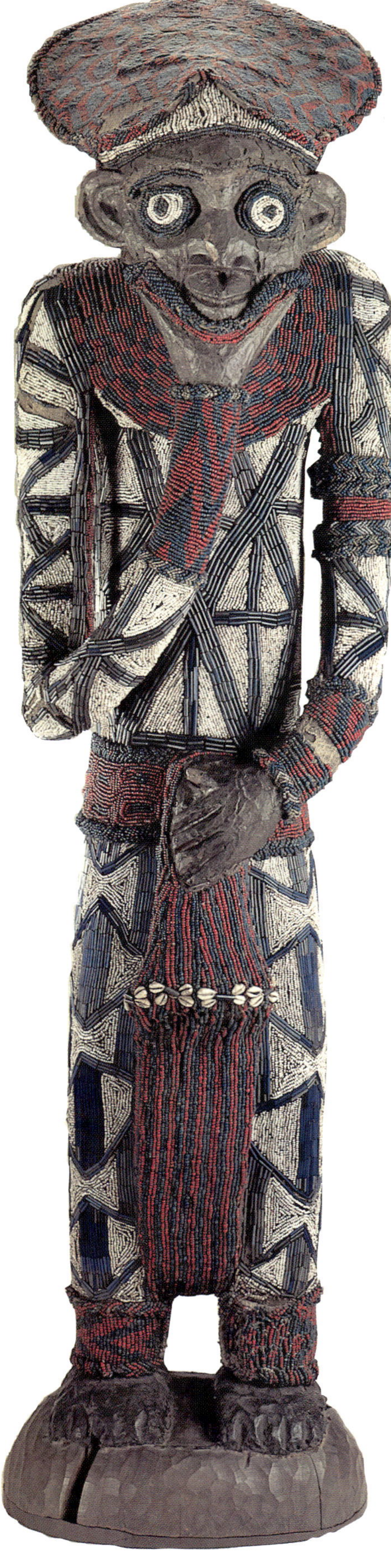

Figure 15
Male figure (back)
Photograph by Franko Khoury

Figure 16
Male figure
Photograph by Franko Khoury

to royal might and communicated the wealth, importance, and glory of the kingdom to the subjects and to other kings and inhabitants of the Grassfields region (Geary 1993).[22]

The figure is the work of these artists; however, we do not know their identities. Its complex production process involved the use of different precious materials. The artist first created the wood carving. Usually, a Bamum carver began working on a large piece where the tree had been felled. When he had completed the rough carving, the artist and his helpers brought it to his workshop, where he performed the finishing touches. Although scientific analysis has not, as yet, identified the wood used in this figure, it is most likely from the *gbom* tree (*"fromager"* in French, "kapok tree" in English), a variety of hardwood reserved exclusively for the king.

Under the bead embroidery, the figure's carved features are well articulated.[23] Judging by the hands, feet, and face with brass overlay and the way the overlay adheres to the surface, the underlying carving is rather smooth, although—as in all Bamum carvings—the adze marks are still visible. Indeed, beaded nineteenth-century carvings usually have a carefully worked surface, as is evident in sculptures with beaded covers that have been damaged or were lost and never replaced. One example is the figurative handle of a brass gong (Figs. 17, 23), which dates to King Nsangu's rule (Geary 1983b, 45, 192). In more recent beaded works, the underlying carving is often shallow and rough. In the case of new anthropomorphic figures, the bead cover alone—rather than the underlying carving—delineates particular features, such as eyes, noses, and mouths.

After the carver completed the figure, he covered it with a fabric made from the fibers of an indigenous plant. According to scientific analysis, the source of the fibers may be a species or variety of *Linum,* the plant from which flax and linen are produced.[24] Currently, imported cotton fabrics have replaced such indigenous fabric as the backing for bead embroidery. In order to produce a tight cover, pieces of the cloth were stitched together and then attached with pegs. In this figure, small, indigenously produced brass pegs secure the cloth.

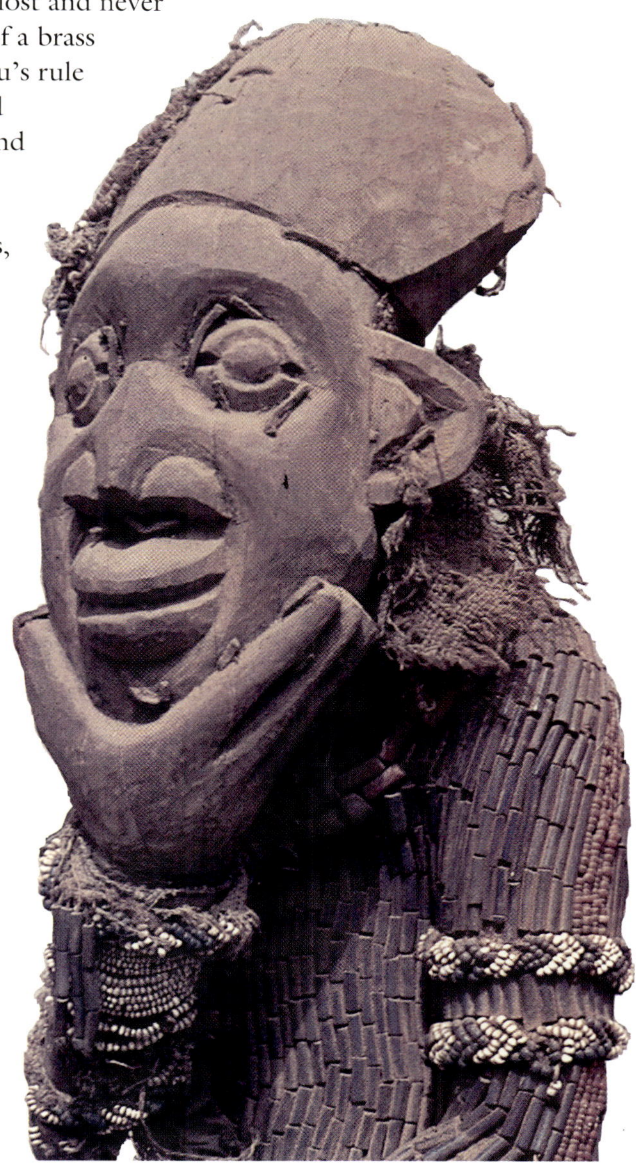

Figure 17
Gong with figurative handle (detail)
19th century
Bamum peoples, Fumban,
Grassfields regions, Cameroon
Brass, wood, cloth, glass beads, cowrie shells
H. 155 cm (61 in); H. of figure 81 cm (31 3/4 in)
Photograph by Christraud M. Geary
Bamum Palace Museum, Fumban, Cameroon

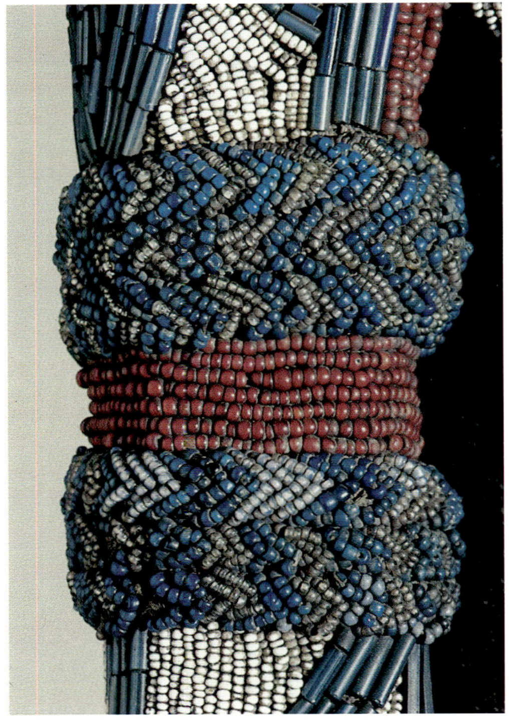

Figure 18
Male figure
(detail of left upper arm with armlet)
Photograph by Franko Khoury

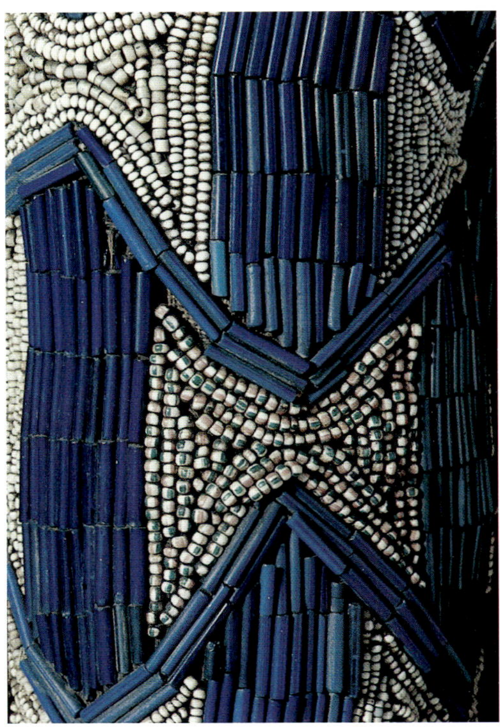

Figure 19
Male figure (detail of left leg)
Photograph by Franko Khoury

A thin brass sheet covers part of the face, neck, hands, and feet and is held in place by similar brass pegs (Fig. 24). This type of brass overlay is typical for pieces that date to the second half of the nineteenth century. Brass, called *lam pütü* (red iron), was a precious and rare commodity in Bamum. Since the sixteenth century, Europeans exported brass in the form of rods, bracelets (also known as *manillas*), basins, and pots to the West African coast (Herbert 1984, 123–53). Brass was in great demand along the coast, and middlemen traded it to the interior. In the nineteenth century, larger quantities reached the Grassfields region mainly from Calabar, a harbor town in Nigeria. Brass, predominantly in the form of heavy spirals, came to Bamum from the west through the neighboring kingdom of Bagham (Geary 1982, 74). In Bamum, only the king had the right to possess and distribute brass.

In addition to brass, peoples living in the Grassfields region of Cameroon valued glass beads imported from Europe. Since the fifteenth century, European merchants have imported glass beads from Italy, Bohemia (now the Czech Republic), and The Netherlands to the West African coast. A network of middlemen traded beads to peoples farther inland. By the nineteenth century, rulers of the Cameroon Grassfields had access to beads and controlled their distribution. Beads served as personal adornment and as a medium to enhance wooden sculptures. In some parts of the Grassfields region, beads became a currency (Warnier 1985, 88).

As a next step in the production of the figure, bead artists carefully applied thousands of small, round or tubular beads to the linenlike fabric (Figs. 11–14). They strung beads on threads and then attached the rows of beads to the figure by sewing approximately every fifth bead to the cloth. This technique is referred to as the "lazy-stitch" method.

Beading wooden sculpture is unique to the Grassfields region of Cameroon, where it is practiced to this day. In this art tradition, the beaded cover becomes an integral and important element of the work of art. In the case of the sculpture under examination, beads indicate and highlight elements of dress and adornment, including a loin cloth, a headdress, bracelets, and a collar. Additionally, the artists elaborated the bead cover with two-dimensional motifs, which are part of an intricate iconography.

The Bamum bead artists used two types of beads in the embroidery of this figure. Small, round or oblate seed beads of no more than three millimeters (1/8 inch) in diameter came in many different colors and are called *memmi* in the Bamum language (Figs. 11–14). Tubular beads (*ntam*) as long as 2.7 centimeters (1-1/8 inches) in length (Figs. 11, 12, and 18) were predominantly blue and brownish red (Harter 1992, 6–10). In the past, the Bamum considered these tubular beads to be more valuable than the seed beads (Geary 1983b, 86–88).

An analysis of the bead embroidery of the figure revealed that there are over twenty different varieties of beads (DeCorse 1993). Three types of seed beads dominate. The

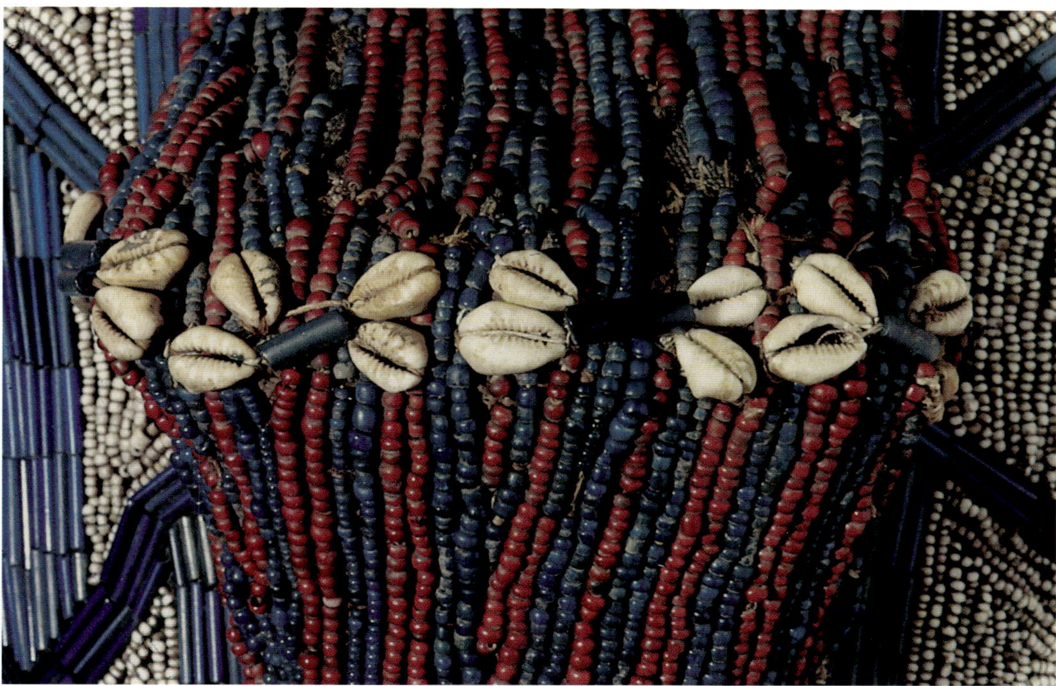

Figure 20
Male figure (detail of loin cloth)
Photograph by Franko Khoury

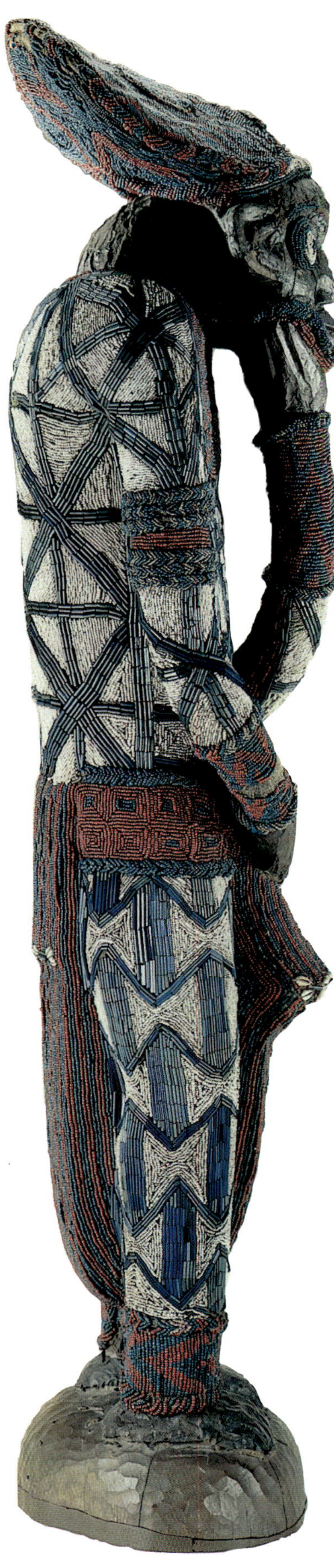

first type—red, round or oblate seed beads—adorn the ankles, belt, loin cloth, collar, face, and headdress of the figure (Fig. 14). These beads contrast with blue, round or oblate seed beads, the second type (Fig. 14). Finally, white, round or oblate seed beads are visible on the torso (Fig. 12). Blue tubular beads embellish the torso, legs, and arms of the figure (Figs. 18, 19). An examination of the patina of the bead cover and the few areas of repair indicates that the vast majority of the beads are part of the original work. The restrained color scheme is common in works created during King Nsangu's rule and during the early years of King Njoya's reign. This color scheme may reflect the aesthetic preferences of the artists; it could also demonstrate the availability of particular beads during this time period. Beaded works produced after the Germans had arrived in Fumban in 1902 tended to be more vivid because the supplies of colorful beads increased. The artists combined reds, blues, greens, yellows, pinks, and other colors. A two-figure throne, which was begun in 1907 (Geary 1983a, 49), is an example of this type of brilliantly colored, beaded object. All of the beads that decorate this figure were available in Europe during the second half of the nineteenth century. Indeed, no bead on the figure is of twentieth-century origin.

Still, using beads to determine when a beaded object was created is not always an accurate method; the use of nineteenth-century beads, for example, does not necessarily mean that a sculpture is a nineteenth-century work. Grassfields bead embroiderers engaged in the common practice of removing older beads from other beaded objects to embroider new pieces. However, the prolific use of four bead types in the case of the beaded figure in the National Museum of African Art suggests that these beads were available in large quantities at the time the figure was embroidered and indicates that these beads were not stripped from other objects (DeCorse 1993, 3). When artists recycled beads from other pieces, they generally used a larger variety of beads because their supplies consisted only of those taken from existing beaded objects of varying sizes.

In addition to beads, Bamum artists applied several cowrie shells to adorn the figure's loin cloth (Fig. 20). Indeed, bead artists in the Grassfields region commonly combined beads and cowrie shells in their embroidery. They drilled small holes through the centers of the cowrie shells and affixed the shells with thread. White cowrie shells contrast in size, color, and texture with the small seed beads and may delineate and highlight particular elements of the beaded design.

Like beads, cowrie shells were imported. They originated in the Indian Ocean, and middlemen traded them across Africa. In

Figure 21
Male figure (side)
Photograph by Franko Khoury

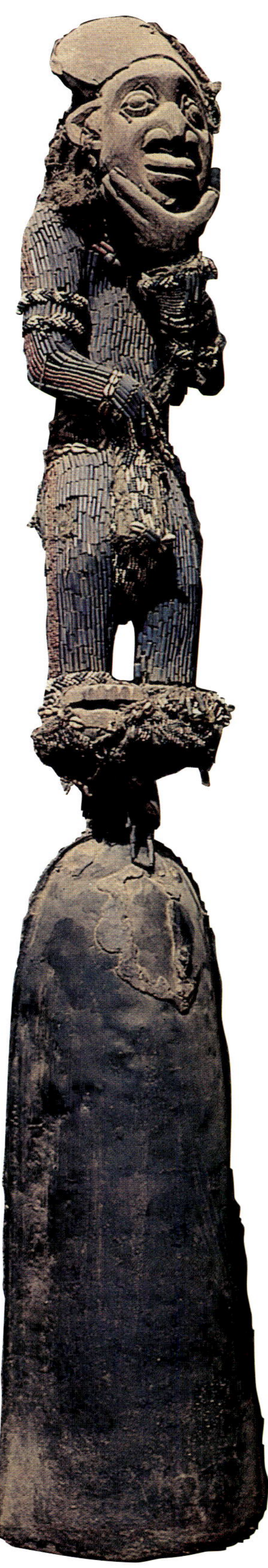

the nineteenth century, Hausa merchants introduced cowrie shells to the Grassfields region from the north (Johnson 1970). By the middle of the nineteenth century, when large quantities of cowrie shells reached the Grassfields region, they had become a widely accepted currency (Warnier 1985, 88). The Bamum word for cowrie shells, *mbuum*, has come to mean "money" and now refers to the modern currency in Cameroon. Like beads, cowrie shells alluded to wealth and to the king's ability to accumulate riches.

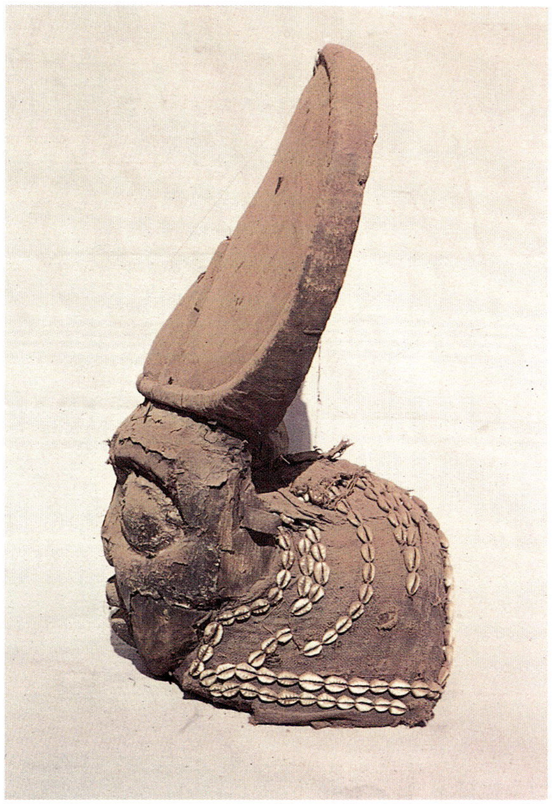

Figure 22
Helmet mask (side)
19th century
Bamum peoples, Fumban, Grassfields region, Cameroon
Brass, cloth, wood, cowrie shells
H. 58 cm (22 3/4 in)
Photograph by Christraud M. Geary
Bamum Palace Museum, Fumban, Cameroon

Figure 23
Gong with figurative handle
Photograph by Christraud M. Geary

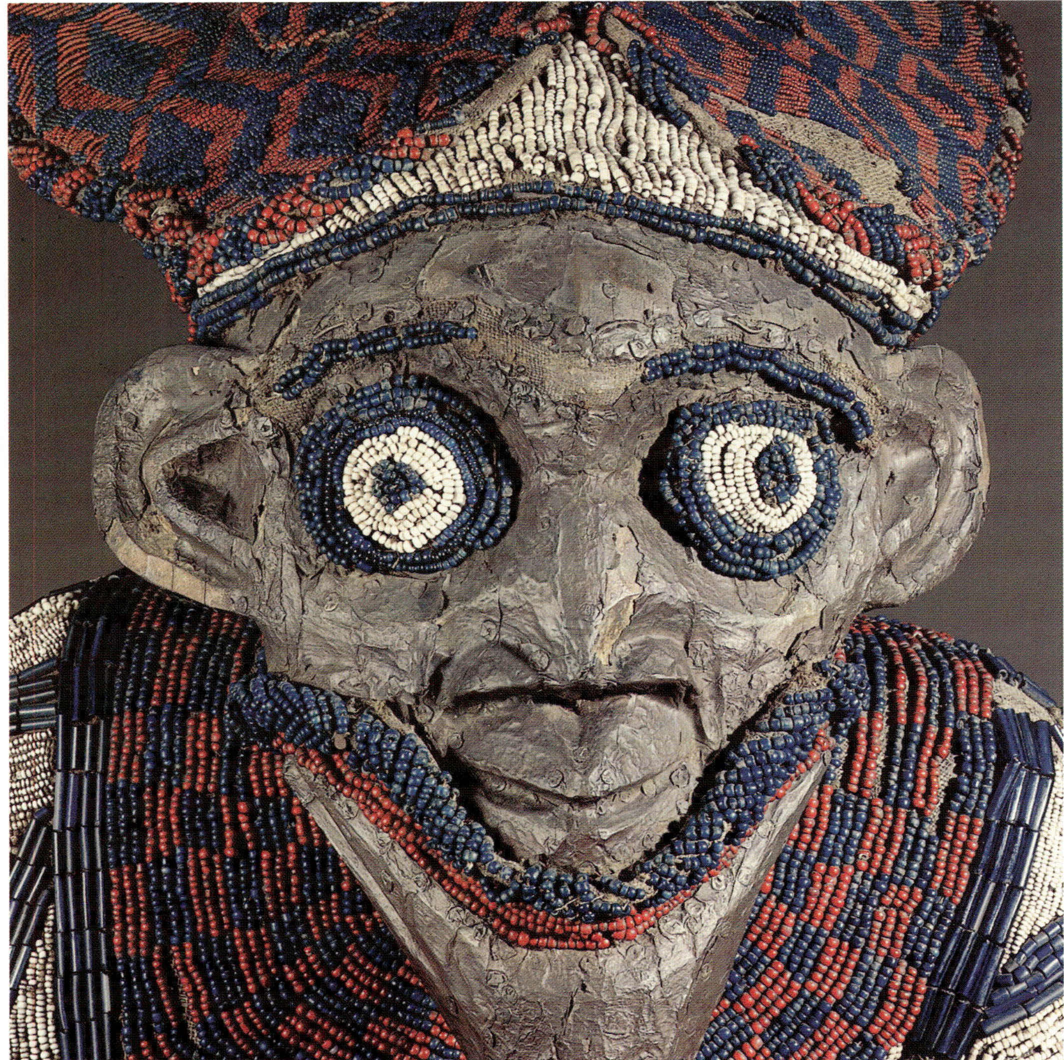

Figure 24
Male figure (detail of face)
Photograph by Franko Khoury

Stylistic Characteristics

Among beaded art works from Bamum, this sculpture is one of few large, free-standing male figures. Others of comparable size and style are usually part of larger works of art, such as beaded thrones (Figs. 8, 26). In another case, a beaded male figure forms the handle of royal ceremonial gong that is in the collection of the Bamum Palace Museum (Figs. 17, 23).

Tall male and female sculptures without beaded covers that formed figurative pillars also resemble the figure (Fig. 27). These pillars adorned the front and some interior courtyards of the royal palace during several years of King Njoya's rule. Such figurative

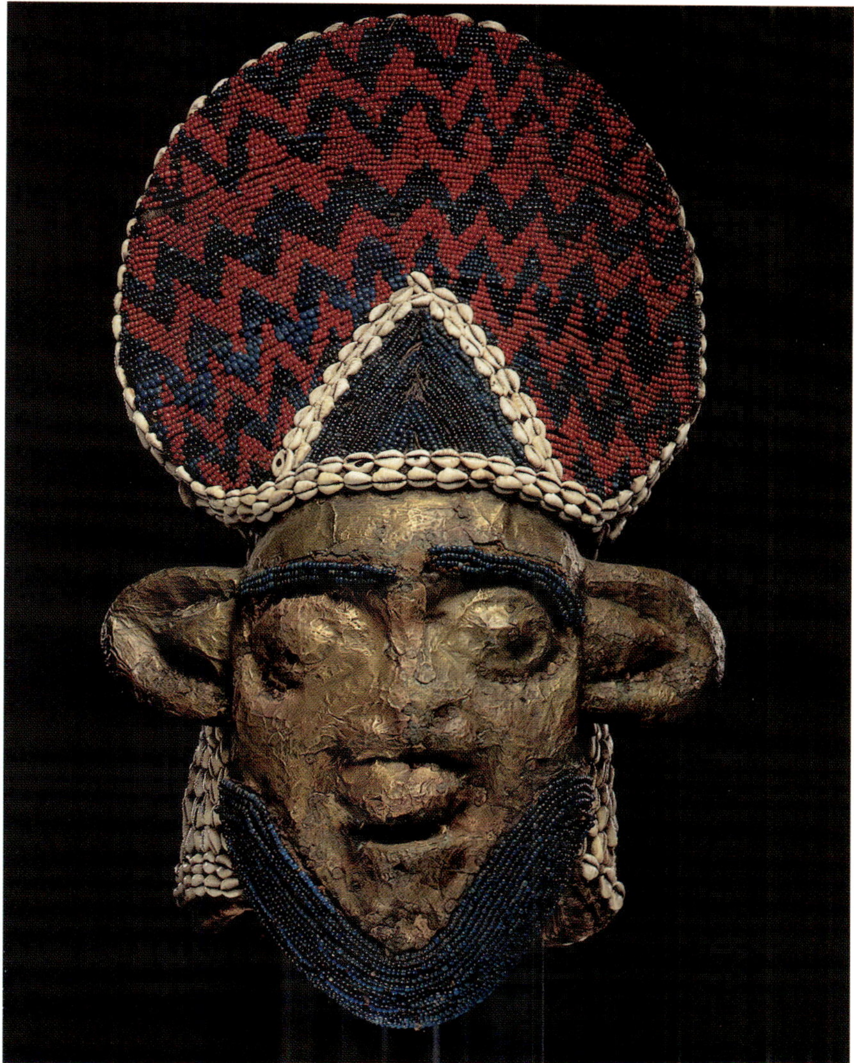

Figure 25
Helmet Mask
19th century
Collected in Bamum by Franz and Marie-Pauline Thorbecke in 1912
Bamum peoples, Fumban, Grassfields region, Cameroon
Brass, wood, glass beads, cowrie shells, cloth
H. 60 cm (23 3/4 in)
Photograph by Jutta Meirer
Courtesy Völkerkundliche Sammlungen im Städtischen Reiss-Museum
Mannheim, Germany; No. IV Af 4888

pillars embellishing palaces were also common among the Bamileke and other neighbors of the Bamum.[25] Dated historical photographs reveal that the first figurative pillars were in place no earlier than 1910; thus, they are more recent than the figure (Ochsner 1993). By 1912, the whole palace façade and several interior courtyards were adorned. Unfortunately, this palace burned down in 1913, and the figurative pillars were not replaced in later buildings.

All sculptures that resemble the figure at the National Museum of African Art were executed in the distinct style of the artists who worked in the palace's workshop. Their body shapes range from heavy set to elongated; their legs are often slightly bent at the knees, and their arms are tightly held to their torsos. The head often sits directly on the torso, and there is no indication of a neck. Many male figures, especially those in the pillars that adorned the palace façade, assume a particular pose: their left hands touch their chins and their right hands rest on the belts that hold their loin cloths in place (Fig. 27).

Within these stylistic conventions, slight variations allow scholars to attribute works to different hands. A comparison of the beaded male figure that forms the handle for the brass gong (Figs. 17, 23), which very likely dates to the rule of King Nsangu (1870s and 1880s), and the sculpture under discussion (Figs. 15, 16) is particularly instructive, for the works were clearly created by different artists. Immediately obvious are the different proportions of the two sculptures. Most male figures, like that of the royal gong, have rounded, short bodies with heavy heads. The figure in the collection of the National Museum of African Art, however, has an elongated, erect, and angular body.

An elongated and rather angular female figure, which is in the collection of the Palace Museum in Fumban (Fig. 26), compares favorably to the sculpture in the National Museum of African Art and shares the same restrained color scheme. This figure has been attributed to the rule of King Nguwuo, a usurper of the Bamum throne who reigned in the 1850s and 1860s, until he was overthrown by the legitimate heir, King Nsangu (Geary 1983b, 112–13, 156; Harter 1986, 163–64). This sculpture is part of a large royal throne and, measured from the knees up, is approximately 140 centimeters (55 inches) in height.

One interesting observation pertains to the execution of the arms of both the female throne figure (Fig. 26) and the figure in the collection of the National Museum of African Art (Fig. 16). In these pieces, the arms are clearly separated from the torsos, whereas in the gong figure the arms are held closely to the torso (Figs. 17, 23). In the figures of the Bamum pillars, which are more recent, the arms actually merge with the torsos (Fig. 27). The similarities between the sculpture at the National Museum of African Art and the throne figure in the Bamum Palace Museum suggest that the works may have been produced during the same time period—that is, in the 1850s to 1880s—perhaps even by the same hand.

The facial features of the Bamum figure in the National Museum of African Art resemble those of the other male figures; however, its face is slightly more triangular than other figures' typically oval faces (Fig. 24). The rather broad area of the large round eyes, accentuated by white and blue beads applied in a circular pattern, merges into large, semicircular ears with triangular insets. Blue seed beads form the eyebrows. The bridge of

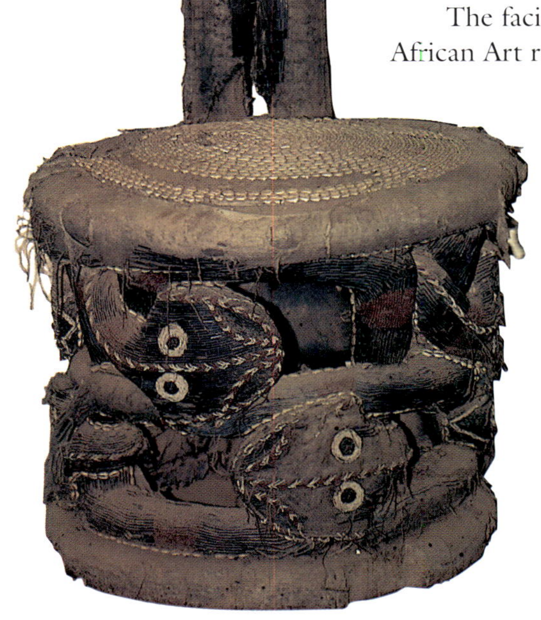

Figure 26
Royal beaded throne with female figure, attributed to King Nguwuo's rule (ca. 1850 to 1865–72)
Bamum peoples, Fumban, Grassfields region, Cameroon
Wood, cloth, glass beads, cowrie shells
H. 208 cm (81 3/4 in); H. of figure 140 cm (55 in)
Photograph by Christraud M. Geary
Bamum Palace Museum, Fumban, Cameroon

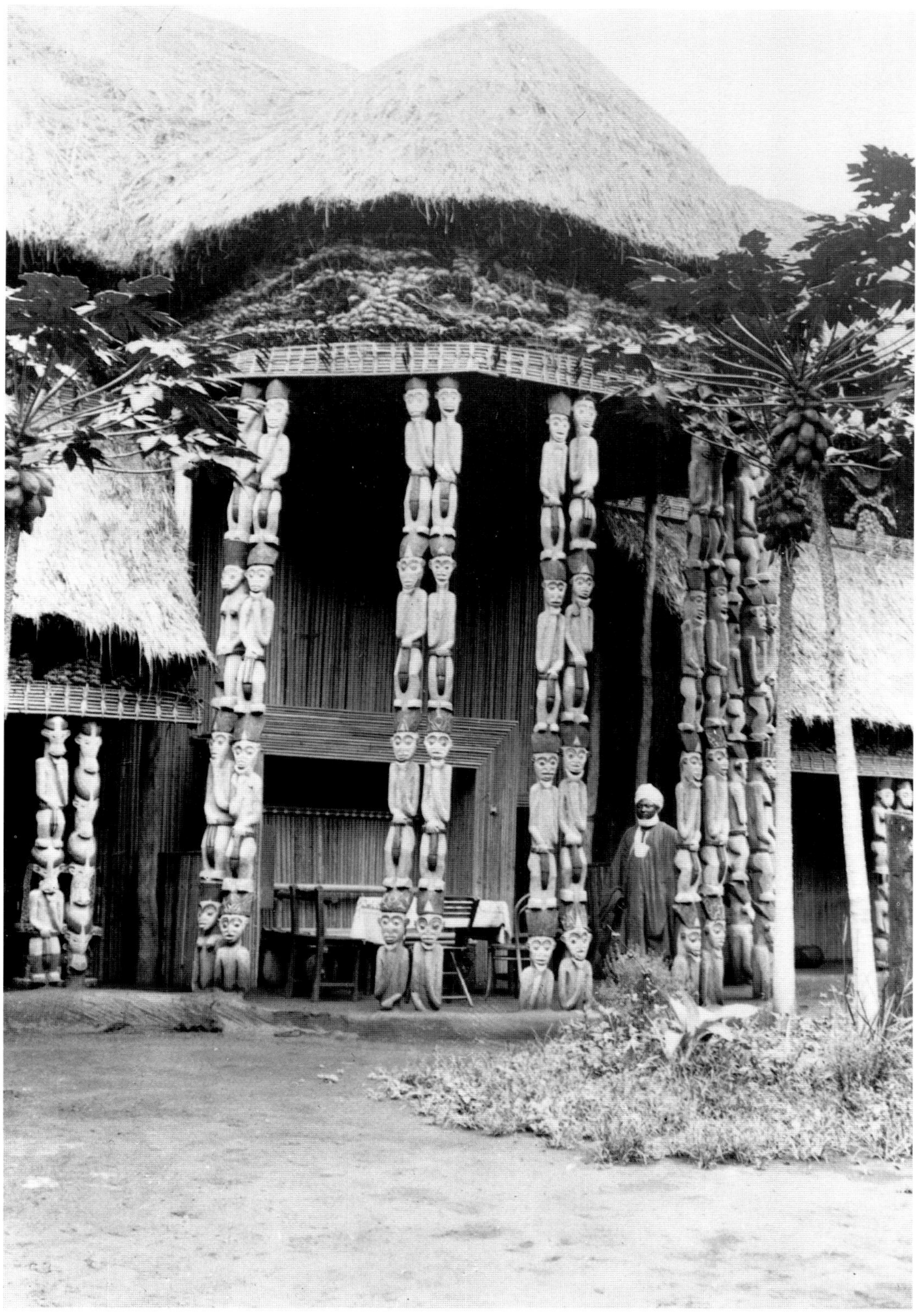

Figure 27
King Njoya in the audience courtyard of the palace
Photograph by Rudolf Oldenburg, ca. 1912
Courtesy Museum für Völkerkunde Vienna, Austria; No. 49878

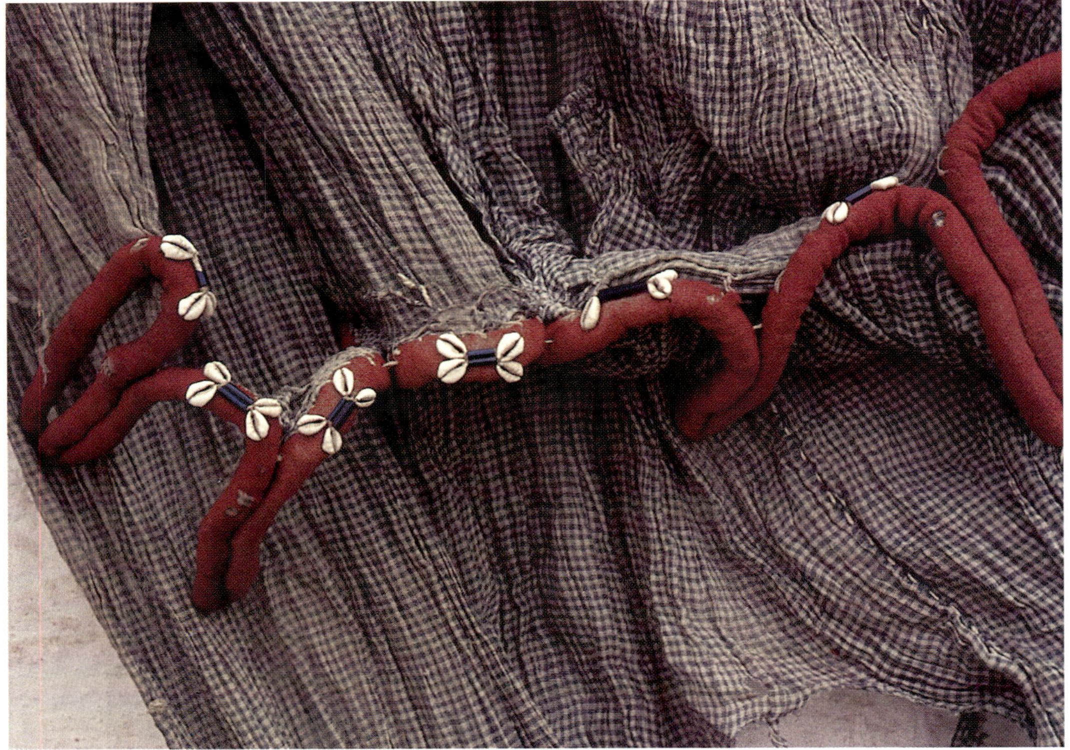

Figure 28
Loin cloth (detail)
Bamum peoples, Fumban, Grassfields region, Cameroon
European cloth, fiber, glass beads, cowrie shells
Photograph by Christraud M. Geary
Bamum Palace Museum, Fumban, Cameroon

the nose is flat, and the nostrils flare. The mouth is narrow and protrudes. A beaded beard, a conventionalized characteristic of all male figures, frames the chin.

This brass-covered face shares similarities with those of other nineteenth-century pieces, such as a male helmet mask in the collection of the Reiss Museum in Mannheim, Germany (Fig. 25). The geographer Franz Thorbecke and his wife, Marie-Pauline, purchased this nineteenth-century mask from King Njoya when they visited Bamum in 1912 (Born 1981, 25–26).[26] Like four similar masks in other European and American collections and in the Bamum Palace Museum,[27] this helmet mask was part of the ensemble that performed during the annual *nja* festival in which dancers with human and animal masks re-created and enacted the Bamum universe in visual terms (Geary 1990). The Mannheim mask, like the figure, has a brass facial overlay and displays a restrained red, blue, and white color scheme. Blue strands of beads accentuate the eyebrows and delineate a beard.

Perhaps the most striking resemblance between these nineteenth-century helmet masks and the sculpture in the National Museum of African Art is the shape of the back of their heads. In profile, all anthropomorphic *nja* helmet masks show characteristically flat faces and slightly curved headdresses (Fig. 22). A rounded helmet (i.e., the back of

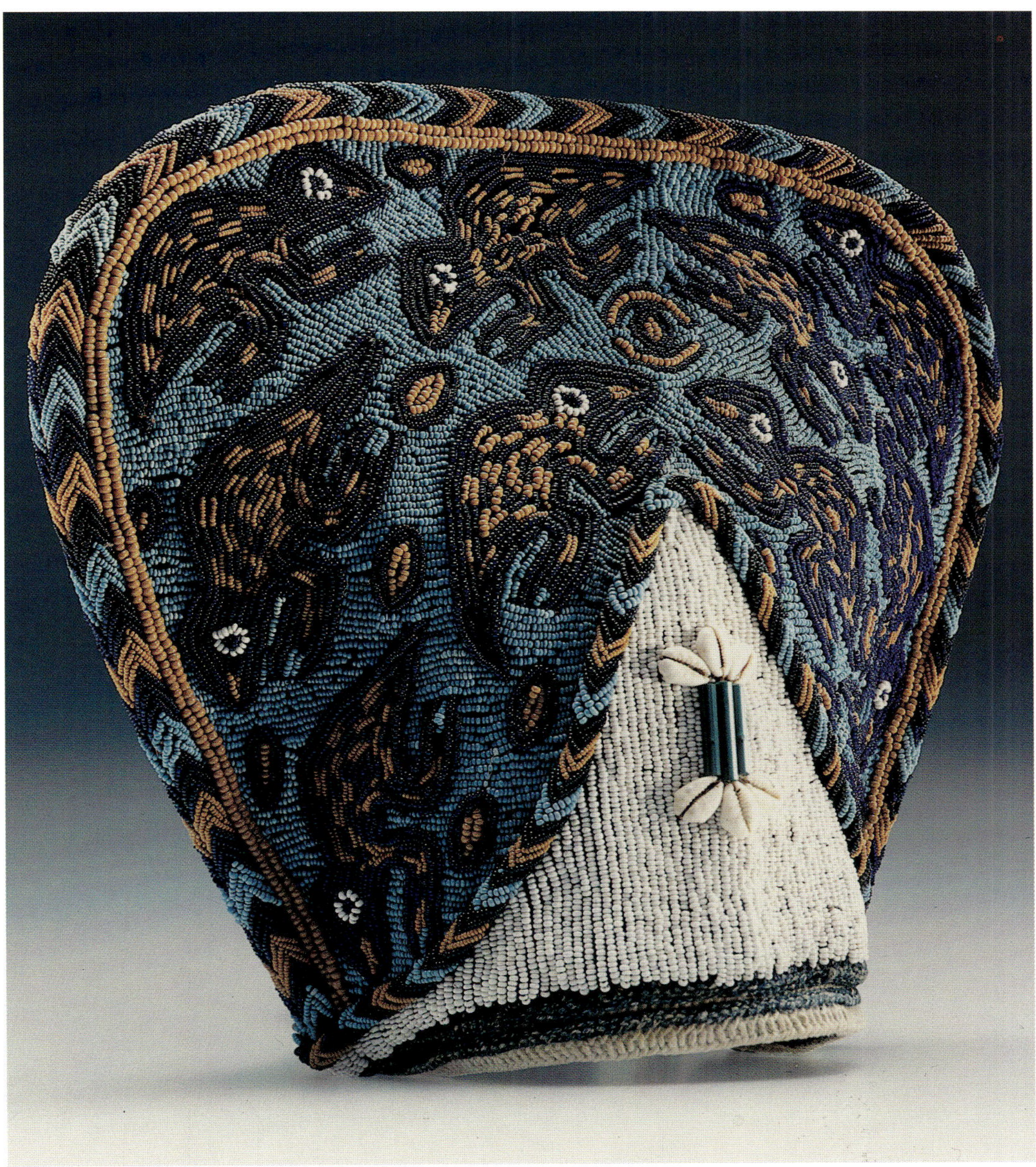

Figure 29
Royal headdress *(mpelet)*
19th century
Bamum peoples, Fumban, Grassfields region, Cameroon
Raffia, fiber, cotton, glass beads, cowrie shells
H. 36 cm (14 3/4 in)
Photograph by Erik Hesmerg
Courtesy Museum für Völkerkunde Berlin, Germany; No. III C 33343, gift of King Njoya

the head) projects to the rear of these masks. From a side perspective (Fig. 21), the figure's neck resembles the backs of these helmet masks. It almost seems as if such a mask has been affixed to the torso.

A similarly structured neck can be seen in the female throne figure attributed to the rule of King Nguwuo (Fig. 26). This execution of the neck seems to be characteristic of nineteenth-century anthropomorphic sculpture. Indeed, in later sculptures, the transition from shoulders to head is treated differently. It is either a flatter, more representational rendering of the neck, as in a pillar carved around 1910 for the palace façade (Fig. 32), or naturalistic, as in the figure of a warrior, created in the 1920s, that is depicted in Figure 35.

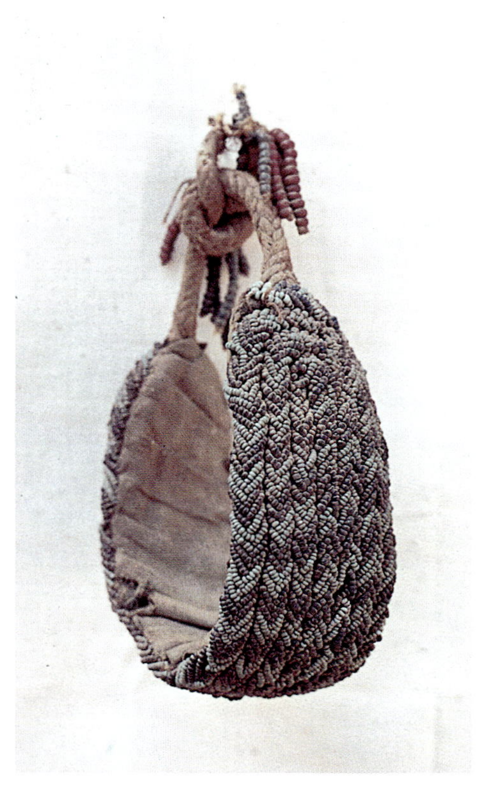

Figure 30
Beaded bracelet
19th century
Bamum peoples, Fumban, Grassfields region, Cameroon
Glass beads, fiber, cotton
L. 27 cm (10 1/2 in)
Photograph by Christraud M. Geary
Bamum Palace Museum, Fumban, Cameroon

Clothing and Adornment

Clothing and adornment of the figure represent the typical attire the king or a prominent Bamum courtier would have worn during festive occasions in the second half of the nineteenth century. Although Islamic full dress replaced this attire shortly before 1900, when the Bamum king and court converted to Islam, this style of pre-Islamic dress is commonly depicted in many carvings to this day.

Among the elements of nineteenth-century, high-status clothing were belts (*nkwom*), which were embroidered with beads for royalty (Geary 1983b, 158). On this sculpture, the wide belt is clearly delineated with red and blue beads. The belt held a loin cloth (*lüöm*) in place. Bamum of the palace and the elite wore cotton cloths imported from the north, as well as expensive and rare European fabrics imported from the coast (Geary 1983b, 101). The edges of the loin cloths were often decorated with cowrie shells and bead ornaments (Fig. 28). Indeed, similar cowrie shell and bead ornaments, with blue tubular beads strung among four cowrie shells, embellish the figure's loin cloth (Fig. 20).

The figure's headdress represents a type called *mpelet,* which was embroidered with beads. This type of headdress was reserved for royalty, high-ranking royal servants, and court officials. It was part of ceremonial dress (Geary 1983b, 103). Several examples of

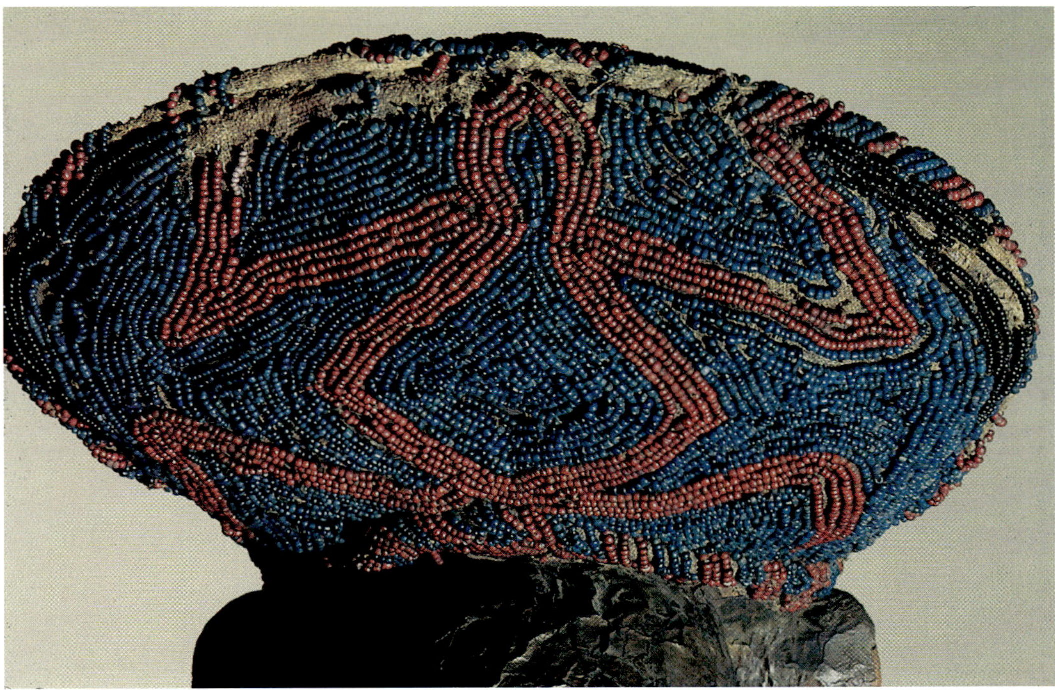

Figure 31
Male figure (detail of headdress)
Photograph by Franko Khoury

such headdresses in the Bamum Palace Museum and in museum collections around the world indicate how these headdresses were made (Fig. 29). A lateral frame holds two rigid fiber pieces in place: one in the front and the other in the back. Bead embroiderers covered these pieces with cotton cloth and brilliantly colored beads. The triangular inset at the front of the headdress is typical of the *mpelet* headdresses. Geometric or zoomorphic designs usually embellish the front and back of these headdresses.

The figure wears rich jewelry, such as wide bracelets (*nsa'mbu*), that is rendered in bead embroidery. Such jewelry was a common nineteenth-century adornment for high-ranking men (see Fig. 30). Beads also delineate armlets and anklets (Fig. 19). Finally, the decorative element around the neck of the figure probably represents a type of broad, flat, cloth-backed bead collar (*kieme*), which was also part of elite attire (Geary 1983b, 166).

Iconography of the Beadwork

Through their beadwork, the artists embellished the figure with rich, two-dimensional designs, which are either stylized representations of animals or are geometric. There are two animal motifs on the figure: the spider motif and the frog motif.[28] The spider motif embellishes the figure's torso (Fig. 12). The frog motif is seen in two different configurations. A representational rendition on the back of the headdress shows the outline of the frog and its head and legs (Fig. 31); the other rendition, on the figure's legs, is more stylized but is still recognizable (Fig. 18).

This use of zoomorphic motifs alludes to the importance of animals in the Bamum system of thought. Like other peoples in the region, the Bamum had complex conceptualizations of the world in which animals assumed symbolic significance (Njiassé-Njoya 1981, 124–56) [29] Indeed, in many African societies, animals constitute primordial metaphors and foster references to many different domains (Ben-Amos 1976; Douglas 1975). Animals' behaviors and physical characteristics, which can be perceived as parallel to human traits, can define what constitutes the nonhuman or uncivilized, as well as the more-than-human or spiritual, realms (Ben-Amos 1976, 243).

Peoples in the Grassfields region perceived the animal world in hierarchical terms that were similar to those of human society. The leopard, serpent, and elephant were all royal referents. The actual beasts, when hunted and killed, and the right to display these motifs were reserved for the king. Their qualities of fierceness, strength, and leadership were seen as analogous to the regal qualities of a powerful king.

Other animals, including the spider and the frog, had different places in this hierarchy, and commoners were allowed to display these motifs. In Grassfields symbolism, frogs—like other animals—have special, intriguing characteristics. Their moisture and suppleness, as well as their ability to propagate rapidly, connote femininity and allude to fecundity. The Bamum also consider frogs to be clever, and frogs are the heroes in many fables (Rein-Wuhrmann 1925, 130–31, 139).

The bold, blue and white geometrical designs on the torso of the figure represent the spider (*ngam*) in stylized forms (Fig. 12). Like the frog motif, representations of the spider in Bamum art can range from the representational to the highly stylized. The reference here is to a particular spider, the earth spider (*Heteroscodra crassipes*).[30] This animal was wisdom incarnated for it played an important part in divination.

Like the frog, the earth spider plays an important role in Bamum culture. Before the majority of the Bamum converted to Islam, they believed in the existence of numerous deities (*nyinyi*) and evil forces (*paghüm*). If misfortune or disease befell a person, he consulted a diviner (*mfon ngam*, literally "king of the spider") who would explore the cause and provide medicine to protect the afflicted from the *paghüm* (Njiassé-Njoya 1981, 140–41). In their divination, these specialists used earth spiders, which burrow holes in the ground. Bamum diviners captured these spiders when they found them in the bush and transferred them to new holes behind their houses. They then covered the holes with clay pots. When a client needed divination, the specialist lifted the pot and placed around the hole a set of small sticks and pieces, all of which were marked and had particular meanings. He then replaced the pot. When the spider left its hole to hunt, it inadvertently moved the small pieces. Subsequently, the diviner uncovered the hole and interpreted the meaning of the new configurations, which foretold the client's future or revealed the reasons for his troubles. The diviner then advised his client about appropriate action (Paré 1956; Rein-Wuhrmann 1925, 138–39).

The earth spider possesses unique qualities and demonstrates particular behaviors that intrigue the Bamum. Because the spider lives underground, it forms a link with the deceased ancestors, who—the Bamum, like other peoples in the Grasssfields region, believe—also dwell in a subterranean realm. In this underground realm, the ancestors maintain the social ranks they had in life and are able to support or interfere with the affairs of the living. The earth spiders' proximity to the ancestors' realm forms a connection between the domains of the living and the deceased.

Other motifs on the figure are associated with important concepts in Bamum thought. The figure's bracelets, armlets, and anklets (Fig. 19) display the zigzag configuration of the "spear motif" (*nja'anku*). Spears were important weapons in warfare, an activity in which the Bamum engaged frequently during the nineteenth century, and the motif alludes to Bamum prowess in war. Finally, geometric motifs adorn the front of the headdress, and designs reminiscent of checkerboards embellish the neck ornament and the belt (Figs. 13, 14). Their meanings remain enigmatic, or they may be simply decorative.

These motifs made powerful statements about royal might and the Bamum culture. The representation of motifs on the beaded figure conveys distinct messages relating to the Bamum system of thought.

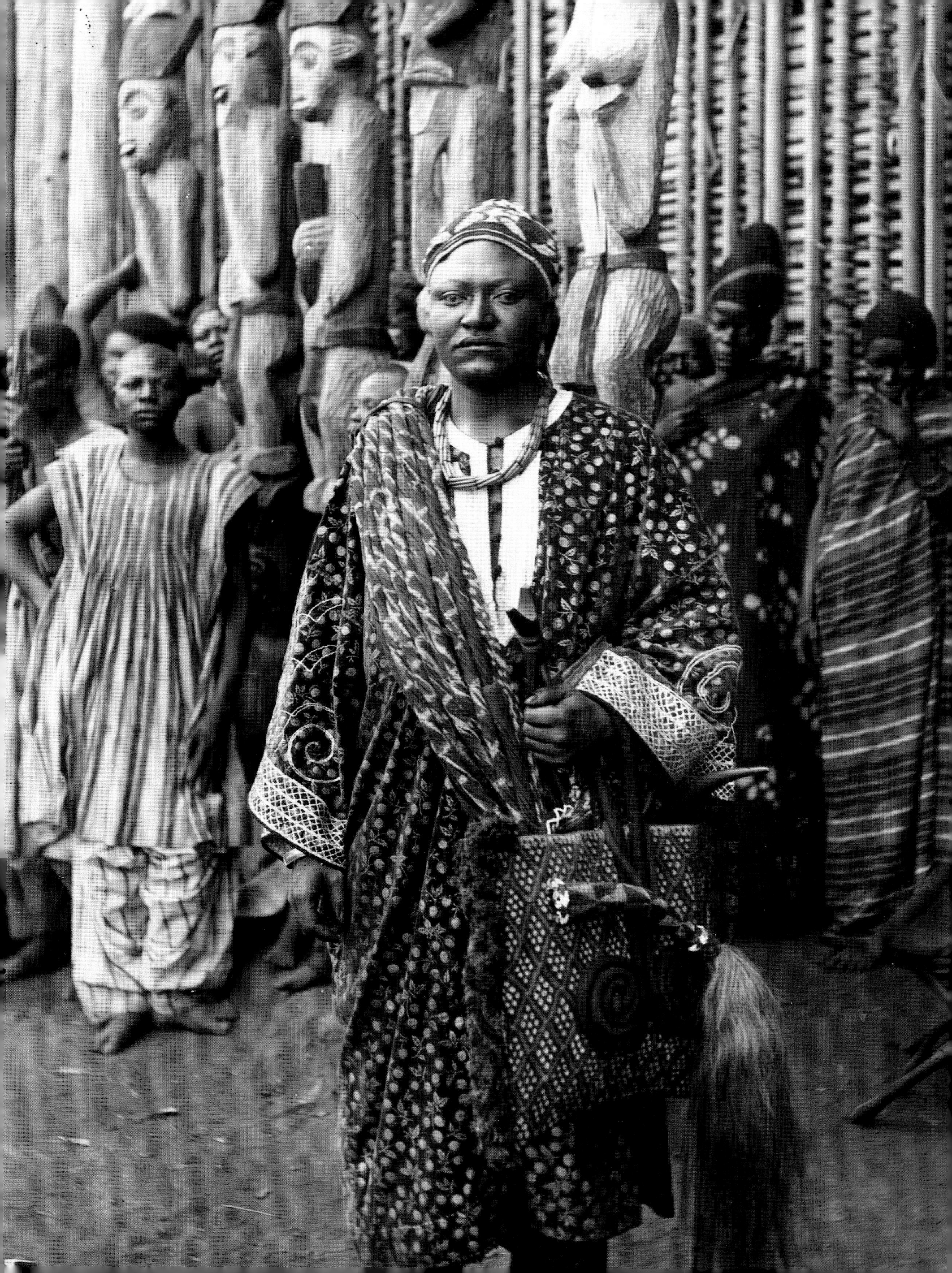

Concluding Thoughts about the Figure's Age, Function, and Meaning

Despite the detailed provenance of this figure and the knowledge of nineteenth-century Bamum art and thought that offers insight into its materials, dress and adornment, style, and iconography, several major questions regarding its actual age, initial use, function, and meaning remain. Here, we can only speculate, for none of these questions can be answered definitively.

Although it is difficult to determine exactly when the figure was created, convincing evidence suggests that it was made in the second half of the nineteenth century—either during King Nguwuo's or King Nsangu's rule in the 1860s to 1880s or during the 1890s in the early years of King Njoya's reign. Analysis of the materials demonstrated that the linenlike cloth backing for the bead work, the brass overlay, and the type of beads used for the embroidery are all typical of nineteenth-century pieces. Moreover, the restrained color scheme of the bead embroidery is common in nineteenth-century works of art, such as the mask in Mannheim and the throne with the female figure in the Palace Museum in Fumban, which is said to date to the rule of King Nguwuo (1850s and 1860s). In terms of style, the figure compares favorably to other nineteenth-century works, including the beaded female throne figure, several helmet masks danced during royal festivals, and the handle of the gong ascribed to King Nsangu's rule (1870s and 1880s).

One question a Westerner might ask is whether the figure is a portrait commemorating an individual. Indeed, portraiture in Africa is common, although it does not

Figure 32
King Njoya standing in front of the palace during the celebration of a royal festival
Photograph by Marie-Pauline Thorbecke, January 1912
Courtesy Rautenstrauch-Joest-Museum Cologne, Germany; No. 19334

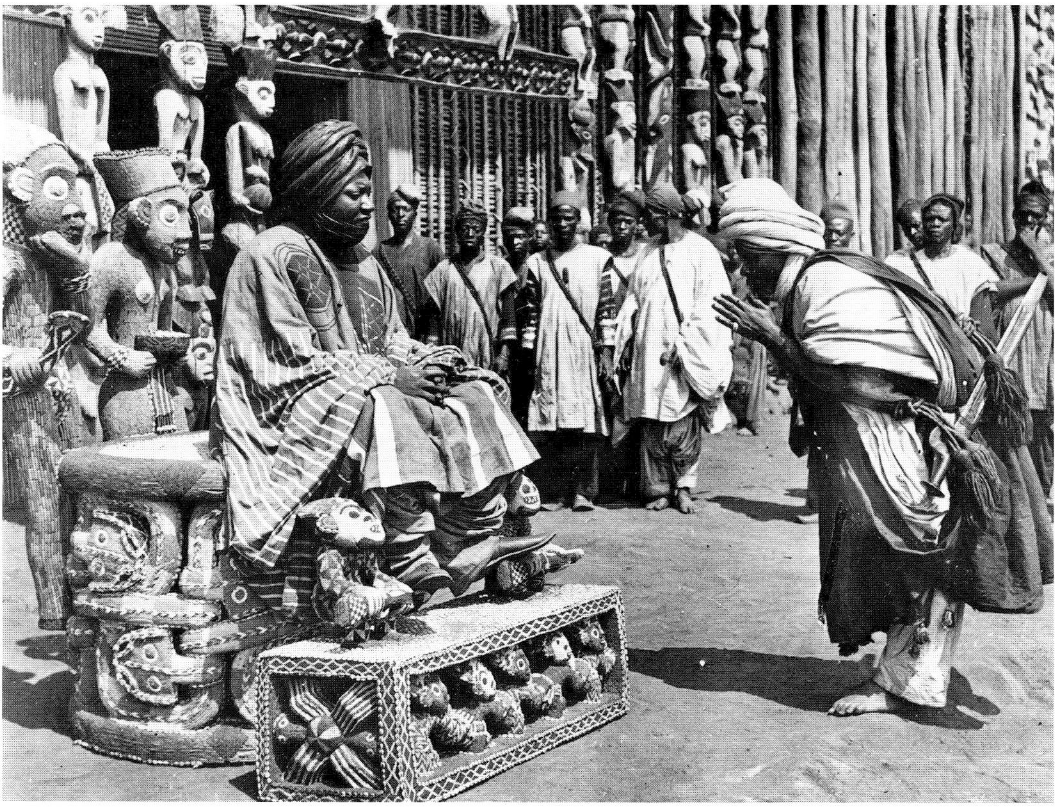

Figure 33
King Njoya giving an audience in front of his palace
Photograph by Marie-Pauline Thorbecke, January 1912
Courtesy Rautenstrauch-Joest-Museum Cologne, Germany; No. 19336

follow the same conventions as portraiture in the West. In the most common definition in the West, a portrait is the likeness of an individual. However, in an insightful essay on African portraits, Jean Borgatti has shown that in African societies with traditions of portraiture likeness is not of the same importance, although portraits may be representational. Portraits thus may be more frequently identified by the names of the people they depict or by other attributes of the portrayed, ranging from dress and adornment to emblems (Borgatti and Brilliant 1990, 29).

Did the Bamum have a tradition of portraiture in the nineteenth century? We know, of course, that many peoples in the Grassfields region produced royal portraits. There are, for example, the famous portraits of the Bangwa kings, the royal figures from Batouffam, and the royal beaded portraits from the Kom kingdom (Geary 1986; Harter 1986, 54–62). In all instances, these sculptures did not aspire to physical likeness. Rather, naming and rendering of royal regalia indicated that the sculptures were portraits. There is some evidence that royal portraiture existed in Bamum, at least in this century. A mask in the Bamum Palace Museum supposedly represents King Mbuembue (Geary 1983b, 202). Another portrait, also in this Bamum Palace Museum, depicts a warrior (Fig. 35). A representational brass sculpture, cast in the 1980s, commemorates King Njoya.

Is this figure a royal portrait? The analysis of dress, adornment, and headdress certainly supports this assumption. However, while this interpretation cannot be dismissed, it seems unlikely given the posture of the sculpture. This position—the left hand of the figure touching the bearded chin and the right hand placed on the belt that holds the loin cloth—is a conventional pose of many male Bamum sculptures. Examples include the male figures on the wooden pillars of the palace (Fig. 27) and on the handle of the brass gong (Figs. 17, 23). I suggest that this gesture represents the typical position assumed by the Bamum in the presence of the king. When talking to the king, men respectfully bow their heads and speak through their raised hands because no one is permitted to look at or address the king directly (Fig. 33). The king is sacred and commands highest respect and reverence from his subjects. The placement of the right hand on the belt that holds the loin cloth also alludes to proper behavior for it indicates composure and restraint in front of the king. Was the individual portrayed—if the figure is indeed a portrait—a Bamum noble man, a royal retainer?

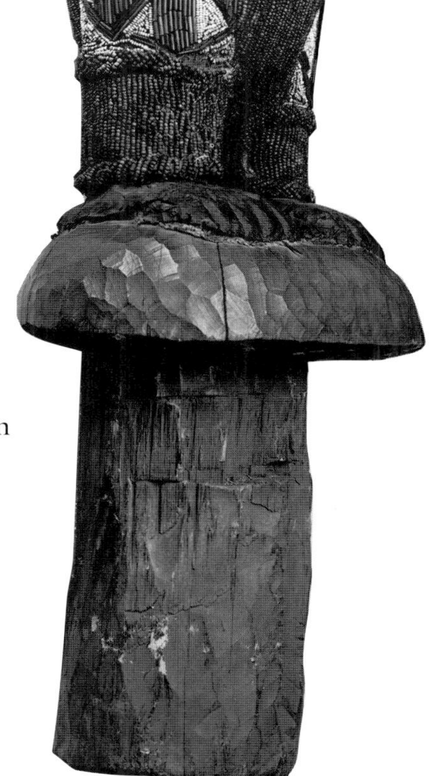

Figure 34
Male figure (detail of pole-like extension)
Photograph by Franko Khoury

Another characteristic of the figure, the pole-like extension, may in fact support the assumption that it is a portrait (Fig. 34). A wooden male figure in the Bamum Palace Museum—which, although not covered with beads, is of comparable size (150 centimeters or 59 inches)—has a similar extension (Fig. 35). King Njoya commissioned this particular sculpture in the second decade of this century to commemorate *Nji* Nagham, an accomplished warrior and vigorous dancer who had served under Njoya's father, King Nsangu. When members of the warrior's association (*mbansie*) met at the palace, they planted the figure in the ground and danced in proud remembrance of one of their own (Geary 1983b, 143–44, 204). Was the museum's sculpture created for a similar purpose and used in a similar context? Does it indeed depict a high-ranking Bamum who had distinguished himself and whose commemorative portrait was displayed during important events at the court? This question remains without an answer.

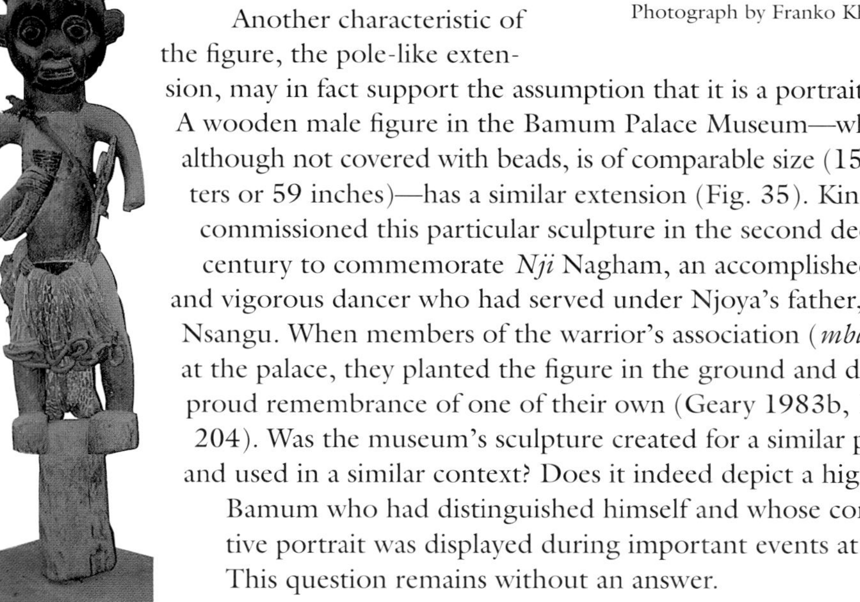

Figure 35
Warrior statue
Bamum peoples, Fumban, Grassfields region, Cameroon
Wood, pigment, cloth
H. 193 cm (76 in); H. of figure 150 cm (59 in)
Photograph by Christraud M. Geary
Courtesy Bamum Palace Museum, Fumban, Cameroon

The exact meaning and function of this impressive figure elude us to this day, and they may never be revealed. Yet the extensive examination of written records demonstrates the figure's place in the political history that unfolded during the German colonial period and its movement from Cameroon through Europe and ultimately to the United States. The evidence to date indicates that the piece was made in the second half of the nineteenth century—either during the rules of King Nguwuo or King Nsangu in the 1850s through 1880s or during the early years of King Njoya's rule, when art production at the Bamum court flourished. Despite its enigmatic nature, this beaded male figure is one of the most important works of art from the Bamum kingdom in a museum in the West, and it stands as a wonderful testament to Bamum artistic achievement.

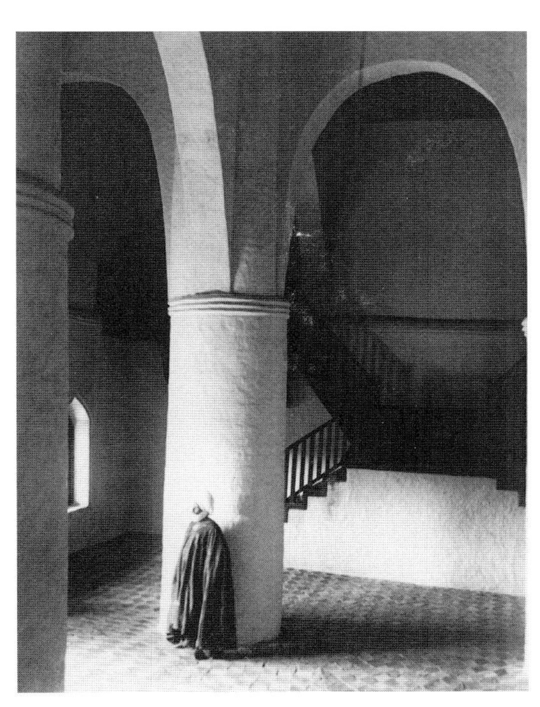

Notes

1 I conducted six months of fieldwork on Bamum art in Fumban under the auspices of a German cultural aid program in 1977 (see Geary 1983b). Shorter stays in Fumban in 1983 and 1984 allowed me to follow up on some questions that were not answered by the earlier research. I thank the Deutsche Forschungsgemeinschaft for supporting this research.

2 Among the outstanding contributions are the writings of Claude Tardits, a French anthropologist, and Aboubakar Njiassé-Njoya, a historian and grandson of King Njoya (Tardits 1980, 1991, 1992; Njiassé-Njoya 1981). Tardits's book, in particular, has become the official reference work for Bamum who want to study their own history and to reenact some of the long-forgotten festivals and rituals.

3 In January 1911, Martin Hohner and Christian Geprägs, missionaries of the Basel Mission Station in Fumban, first mention a short history of Bamum written by King Njoya (Hohner and Geprägs 1911). Geprägs also sent a literal translation of this historical text to his superiors. It is now in the Basel Mission Archive (Geprägs 1911).

4 The Bamum kingdom came under the colonial domination of the Germans in 1902. During the First World War, in 1915, the British drove the Germans out of this part of Cameroon and remained there for a short period of time. The French took control from the British in 1916. Since 1960, when Cameroon became independent, the Bamum kingdom has been part of the Republic of Cameroon, where it forms the Département Bamoum of the West Province.

5 All historical dates given for the precolonial period—that is, for the time before 1902—are based on careful estimates, which are informed by interpretation of Bamum oral traditions and consideration of historical events outside the Bamum kingdom that provide firm dates. Nevertheless, these estimates remain approximate. In some instances, therefore, a span of years indicates the time period within which an event took place.

6 During the Berlin Conference (1884–85), also known as the "Congo Conference," thirteen European nations, with the participation of the United States, divided up the African territories that had come under their domination and decided the future of the African continent. Cameroon, Togo, parts of Eastern Africa, and southwest Africa came under German rule (Mveng 1963, 285–88).

7 All translations from French and German into English were done by the author. The translations of citations from the *Histoire* closely follow the original text and maintain its particular style; the phonetic spellings that occur in this document have been converted for clarity and consistency.

8 The German colonial administration kept accurate records of such gift exchanges. In the German Zentrales Staatsarchiv in Potsdam, there is, for example, a folder entitled "Akten betreffend Geschenke an Häuptlinge pp. in Kamerun und in den Nachbarkolonien, sowie Gegengeschenke vom 30. Mai 1888 bis Juni 1911" (Records concerning gifts to chiefs etc. in Cameroon and in neighboring colonies, as well as return-gifts, from May 30, 1888, to June 1911 [Zentrales Staatsarchiv, Potsdam: RKA 10.01.4102]).

9 Occasional references in collectors' letters to museums permit some insight into the prices that Njoya charged. Bernhard Ankermann, who conducted fieldwork in the Cameroon Grassfields from December 1907 to April 1909, mentions two large drums with heads carved in relief on their bodies. Since these drums sat outside the palace, they were frequently photographed. Njoya apparently wanted 1,000 German marks for both drums (Ankermann 1908c). Evidently, nobody bought them because they remain in the Bamum Palace today. To give some comparisons, at that time, 1.00 U.S. gold dollar equaled 4.20 German gold marks. A German primary school teacher with ten years of service earned an annual salary of 1,650 marks, a bar of soap cost 0.15 to 0.30 marks depending on the quality, and one pound of coffee cost 1.00 to 1.80 marks.

10 In a letter to von Luschan, Glauning mentions that Njoya is pleased to do him any favor he requests and that he is very loyal to the German emperor. He also states that Njoya is a freethinker and a great friend of European culture (H. Glauning 1906b).

11 According to Tardits's estimate, the first war between the Nso and the Bamum, and thus King Nsangu's death, took place between 1885 and 1887 (Tardits 1980, 914).

12 See H. Glauning 1906a for a description of the military campaign and Göhring 1907 for a description of the aftermath and celebration in Fumban.

13 The Bamum writers refer to H. Glauning as "Hauptmann Grared." Similarly, the names of other Germans appear in changed forms.

14 I thank Dr. Hans-Joachim Koloss, curator of the African collections at the Museum für Völkerkunde Berlin, and Dr. Angelika Tunis for letting me study these files. I am particularly grateful to Dr. Koloss for permitting me to publish some of the information contained in these records in this essay.

15 In this letter to von Luschan, Glauning writes:

> In order to ease your mind, I should let you know that the throne of the Bansso [Nso] chief is in my possession and with my personal belongings. The stool is intended for you, and I will have it sent to you as soon as I will return to Germany again for a vacation. Should I, which of course I do not wish to occur, die before that, you can present this letter to my heirs as a quasi will, so that the museum will safely take possession of the stool. (H. Glauning 1907; translated from German)

The current location of the stool is unknown to me.

16 The designation "Muntschi" refers to the Tiv (also known in literature as Munshi or Mitshi), a people living in the Benue State of Nigeria, close to the present-day border of Cameroon and Nigeria. During the German colonial period, the border between the German and British territories was different, and some Tiv actually resided in the German territory.

17 The Glauning family kept some fine Bamum pieces. Two of these, a stool and a ceremonial pipe, were sold in 1928 to Arthur Speyer, an eminent German collector and dealer. In 1979, Speyer's son sold the ceremonial pipe (Musée Barbier-Mueller, Inv. 1018–8) to Jean Paul Barbier. In 1936, Speyer sold the beaded stool (Musée Barbier-Mueller, Inv. 1018–73) to Charles Ratton in Paris. In 1985, Jean Paul Barbier acquired it from Ratton's successor (Perrois 1994, 44). I thank Mrs. Sylvia H. Williams, Director of the National Museum of African Art, for this information.

18 A photograph of the figure also appeared in a book by the English author Albert Calvert. This book was published in 1917, just after the Germans had left Cameroon and the British had taken over part of the territory—before it ultimately fell to the French. The caption reads: "Made by the natives of Bamum" (Calvert 1917, Pl. 109).

19 I am most grateful to Dr. Hans-Joachim Koloss for sending me this information and an excerpt of the file pertaining to the trade.

20 According to Tardits, the Bamum language does not distinguish between artists and craftsmen, although there is a clear sense of the aesthetic qualities of each artist's work (Tardits 1992, 303).

21 *Nji* is the title of the head of a lineage of either royal descent or of nobility.

22 It should be noted that King Njoya released the artists from royal service in the second decade of this century. From then on, they were free to work for a wider clientele, including increasing numbers of foreigners who visited the famed Bamum kingdom. This ultimately led to the creation of the "artisanat," a lively colony along the "street of the artists" in the quarter of Njisse of Fumban.

23 In Bamum sculpture, adze marks are typically visible, although some works, carved very carefully, have smoother surfaces than others.

24 In beaded works dating to the nineteenth and early twentieth centuries, the embroidery is attached to cloth composed of indigenous fibers. In more recent works, the underlying cloth has been produced in Western textile factories. I thank Skip Palenik, senior research microscopist, Microtrace, for his analysis of the fiber samples from this sculpture.

25 Although he may have heard about these palaces earlier, King Njoya first saw such pillars when he traveled to the Cameroon coast in January 1908. King Njoya, a great architect, enjoyed building royal residences and expanding his palace; he always strove to integrate new architectural elements. Inspired by the Bamileke carvings, he may well have commissioned his artists and their apprentices to produce similar pillars.

26 In 1913, the Thorbeckes gave the collection to the Reiss Museum in Mannheim, the hometown of Franz Thorbecke, in return for the town's partial financial support of their research expedition (Born 1981, 4).

27 In addition to the mask in Mannheim, there is a similar mask in a private collection in Switzerland and another in the collection of the Metropolitan Museum of Art (No. 1978.412.569). A fourth mask has been preserved in the Bamum Palace Museum, and a similar piece was displayed in the residence of Sultan Seidou Njimolouh Njoya in 1977 (see also Geary 1990, Figs. 12–14, 16, and 17).

28 In literature, this motif is referred to as either the frog or toad motif (see Harter 1986, 341–43; Northern 1984, 50–53). The Bamum use the French word *crapeau* (toad) as the translation of *ntetuo*. Clearly, all these terms refer to a batrachian, an order of amphibians without tails. I use the term "frog motif."

29 When the majority of the Bamum converted to Islam at the beginning of this century, some of these intricate beliefs were replaced by tenets of the new religion. Thus, we need to draw on historical sources, reconstruction, and parallels with the belief systems of other Grassfields peoples to explore the meanings of some of these motifs.

30 While most scholars identify this spider as an earth spider, two scholars of Grassfields arts offer divergent interpretations. Tardits suggests that, in the case of Bamum royal art, the spider depicted is the "bird spider," which the Bamum king consulted before any risky activity. The spider motif alludes to the rulers' obligations to be cautious and wise (Tardits 1992, 303). Paul Gebauer mentions the "web-weaving" spider in reference to spider motifs on carved ivory tusks from Babanki Tungo, a kingdom near Bamenda. The web-weaving spider was a cherished guest in any home and symbolized peace and protection. Gebauer further mentions that this spider design should not be confused with that depicting the earth spider (Gebauer 1979, 375).

References

"Abschrift zu Bericht Nr. 153." 1906. September 1. *Akten betreffend: Allgemeine Angelegenheiten Kamerun vom September 1905 bis Juni 1906. Verwaltungssachen 12 c.* Zentrales Staatsarchiv, Potsdam, Germany. RKA 10.01 4290.

"Abschrift zu Bericht Nr. 356." 1907a. June 5. *Akten betreffend: Allgemeine Angelegenheiten Kamerun vom April 1907 bis Juni 1908. Verwaltungssachen 12 c nr. 1.* Zentrales Staatsarchiv, Potsdam, Germany. RKA 10.01 4291.

"Abschrift zu Bericht Nr. 356. Militärstation. I. No. 979." 1907b. June 14. *Akten betreffend: Allgemeine Angelegenheiten Kamerun vom April 1907 bis Juni 1908. Verwaltungssachen 12 c nr. 1.* Zentrales Staatsarchiv, Potsdam, Germany. RKA 10.01 4291.

Ankermann, Bernhard. 1908a. Letter to von Luschan. 22 March. Archives of the Museum für Völkerkunde Berlin. No. E.1105/08.

———. 1908b. Letter to von Luschan. 15 May. Archives of the Museum für Völkerkunde Berlin. No. E.1422/08.

———. 1908c. Letter to von Luschan. 19 November. Archives of the Museum für Völkerkunde Berlin. No. E.N.2484/08.

Baumann, Hermann and Lazlo Vajda. 1959. "Bernhard Ankermanns völkerkundliche Aufzeichnungen im Grasland von Kamerun 1907–1909." *Baessler Archiv* N.F. 7(2): 217–317.

Ben-Amos, Paula. 1976. "Men and Animals in Benin Art." *Man* 2(2): 243–52.

Borgatti, Jean and Richard M. Brilliant. 1990. *Likeness and Beyond: Portraits from Africa and the World.* New York: The Center for African Art.

Born, Klaus. 1981. *Skulpturen aus Kamerun: Sammlung Thorbecke 1911/12.* Mannheim: Reiss-Museum.

Calvert, Albert. 1917. *The Cameroons.* London: T. Werner Laurie.

DeCorse, Christopher. 1993. "The Beads of Bamum: Comments on the Beadwork of the Bamum Figure in the National Museum of African Art, Smithsonian Institution, Washington, D.C." Eliot Elisofon Photographic Archives, National Museum of African Art.

Douglas, Mary. 1975. *Implicit Meanings: Essays in Anthropology.* London: Routledge and Kegan Paul.

Eine Reise durch die deutschen Kolonien. 1910. Vol. 2, *Kamerun.* Berlin: Verlag kolonialpolitischer Zeitschriften.

"Ein seltsames Grabdenkmal." 1909. *Kolonie und Heimat* 2(8): 11.

Geary, Christraud M., 1981. "Bamum Thrones and Stools." *African Arts* 14(4): 32–43.

———. 1982. "Casting the 'Red Iron': Bamum Bronzes." In *The Art of Metal in Africa,* ed. Marie-Thérèse Brincard. New York: The African-American Institute.

———. 1983a. "Bamum Two-Figure Thrones: Additional Evidence." *African Arts* 16(4): 46–53.

———. 1983b. *Things of the Palace: A Catalogue of the Bamum Palace Museum in Fumban (Cameroon).* Studien zur Kulturkunde, vol. 60. Trans. Kathleen M. Holman. Wiesbaden: Steiner Verlag.

———. 1986. "Portraiture in the Cameroon Grassfields: A Critical Overview." Paper presented at the Seventh Triennial Symposium on African Art, Los Angeles.

———. 1988. *Images from Bamum. German Colonial Photography at the Court of King Njoya, Cameroon, West Africa, 1902–1905.* Washington, D.C.: National Museum of African Art.

———. 1990. "Photographie als kunsthistorische Quelle. Das *nja* Fest der Bamum (Kamerun) im späten 19. und frühen 20. Jahrhundert." In *Der Sinn des Schönen. Ästhetik, Soziologie und Geschichte der afrikanischen Kunst,* ed. Miklós Szalay. München: Trickster.

———. 1993. "Art and Political Process in the Kingdoms of Bali-Nyonga and Bamum (Cameroon Grassfields)." In *Art in Small-scale Societies: Contemporary Readings,* ed. Richard L. Anderson and Karen L. Field. Englewood Cliffs, New Jersey: Prentice-Hall.

———. 1995. "Art, Politics, and the Transformation of Meaning: Bamum Art in the Twentieth Century." In *African Material Culture,* ed. Mary Jo Arnoldi, Christraud M. Geary, and Kris Hardin. Bloomington: Indiana University Press.

Gebauer, Paul. 1979. *Art of Cameroon.* Portland: The Portland Art Museum in association with the Metropolitan Museum of Art, New York.

Geprägs, Christian. 1911. "Geschichte der Bamum-Könige aus Rifum. Nach den Aufzeichnungen des Königs Njoya." Basel Mission Archive. No. E-10.1.2.

Glauning, Fritz. 1908a. Letter to von Luschan. 6 July. Archives of the Museum für Völkerkunde Berlin. No. E.264/08.

———. 1908b. Letter to von Luschan. September. Archives of the Museum für Völkerkunde Berlin. No. E.1907/08 with 264/08.

Glauning, Hans. 1906a. "Bericht des Hauptmanns Glauning in Bamenda über die Bansso-Expedition." *Deutsches Kolonialblatt:* 705–707.

———. 1906b. Letter to von Luschan. 24 March. Archives of the Museum für Völkerkunde Berlin. No. E.115/06.

———. 1907. Letter to von Luschan. 15 November. Archives of the Museum für Völkerkunde Berlin. No. E.NJ 264/08.

Göhring, Martin. 1907. "Jahresbericht der Station Bamum für das Jahr 1907." 31 January. Basel Mission Archive. No. E-2.25.61.

Harter, Pierre. 1986. *Arts anciens du Cameroun.* Arnouville, France: Arts d'Afrique Noire.

———. 1992. "The Beads of Cameroon." *Beads: Journal of the Society of Bead Researchers* 4: 5–10.

Herbert, Eugenia W. 1984. *Red Gold of Africa: Copper in Precolonial History and Culture.* Madison: University of Wisconsin Press.

Histoire et coutumes des Bamum. 1952. Rédigées sous la direction du Sultan Njoya. Traduction du Pasteur Henri Martin. Mémoires de l'Institut Français d'Afrique Noire, Centre du Cameroun. Série: Population, no. 5.

Hohner, Martin and Christian Geprägs. 1912. "Jahresbericht 1911." 16 January. Basel Mission Archive. No. E-2.34.63.

Johnson, Marion. 1970. "The Cowrie Currencies of West Africa." *Journal of African History* 11(1): 331–53.

Luschan, Felix von. 1908a. Letter to Hermann Glauning. 14 April. Archives of the Museum für Völkerkunde Berlin. No. E.264/08.

———. 1908b. Letter to Ankermann. 19 November. Archives of the Museum für Völkerkunde Berlin. No. E.2129/08.

Mveng, Engelbert. 1963. *Histoire du Cameroun.* Paris: Présence Africaine.

Njiassé-Njoya, Aboubakar. 1981. "Naissance et évolution de l'Islam en pays Bamum (Cameroun)." Thesis (Doctorat de troisième cycle), Université Paris I—Panthéon Sorbonne.

Northern, Tamara. 1984. *The Art of Cameroon.* Washington, D.C.: Smithsonian Institution Traveling Exhibition Service.

Ochsner, Christine. 1993. "Der Koenigspalast von Fumban: Architektur und Bauplastik als Ausdruck von Macht." Seminararbeit. Basel Mission Archive.

Paré, Isaac. 1956. "L'araignée divinatrice." *Etudes Camerounaises* 53: 61–83.

Perrois, Louis. 1994. *Arts royaux du Cameroun.* Geneva: Musée Barbier-Mueller.

Planitz, Edler von der. 1908. Letter to von Luschan. 10 April. Archives of the Museum für Völkerkunde Berlin. No. E.1422/08.

Rein-Wuhrmann, Anna. 1925. *Mein Bamumvolk im Grasland von Kamerun.* Stuttgart: Evanglischer Missionsverlag.

"Report on a trade with Arthur Speyer." 1929. Archives of the Museum für Völkerkunde Berlin. No. E.212/29.

Sandrock, Lieutenant. 1902. "Bericht über den Marsch nach Bafu." 7 July. National Archives, Yaoundé, Cameroon. Fonds Allemands 1/112.

Sydow, Eckart von. 1930. *Handbuch der afrikanischen Plastik.* Berlin: Dietrich Reimer and E. Vohsen.

Tardits, Claude. 1980. *Le royaume Bamoum.* Paris: Armand Colin.

———. 1991. "L'écriture, la politique et le secret chez les Bamoum." Africa (Istituto Italo-Africano) 46(2): 224–39.

———. 1992. "The Kingdom of Bamum (Cameroon)." In *Kings of Africa: Art and Authority in Central Africa,* ed. Erna Beumers and Hans-Joachim Koloss. Maastricht: Foundation Kings of Africa.

Warnier, Jean-Pierre. 1985. Échanges, développement, et hièrarchie dans le Bamenda pré-colonial (Cameroun). Studien zur Kulturkunde, vol. 76. Stuttgart: Franz Steiner Verlag Wiesbaden.

Wenckstern, Lieutenant von. 1907. "Der Kopf des Bamum-Herrschers." *Deutsches Kolonialblatt:* 258–59.

"Zwei Trauerbotschaften." 1908. *Kolonie und Heimat* 1(14):10.